Manhattan
Skyscrapers

Manhattan Skyscrapers

REVISED AND EXPANDED EDITION

Eric P. Nash

PHOTOGRAPHS BY Norman McGrath

INTRODUCTION BY Carol Willis

PRINCETON ARCHITECTURAL PRESS   NEW YORK

PUBLISHED BY
Princeton Architectural Press
37 East 7th Street
New York, NY 10003

For a free catalog of books, call 1.800.722.6657
Visit our website at www.papress.com

Printed and bound in China
08 07 06 05 4 3 2 1

The publisher gratefully acknowledges all of the individuals and organizations that provided photographs for this publication. Every effort has been made to contact the owners of copyright for the photographs herein. Any omissions will be corrected in subsequent printings.

FIRST EDITION
DESIGNER: Sara E. Stemen
PROJECT EDITOR: Beth Harrison
PHOTO RESEARCHERS: Eugenia Bell and Beth Harrison

REVISED AND UPDATED EDITION
PROJECT EDITOR: Clare Jacobson
ASSISTANTS: John McGill, Lauren Nelson, and Dorothy Ball

SPECIAL THANKS TO:
Nettie Aljian, Nicola Bednarek, Janet Behning, Penny (Yuen Pik) Chu, Russell Fernandez, Jan Haux, Clare Jacobson, John King, Mark Lamster, Nancy Eklund Later, Linda Lee, Katharine Myers, Jane Sheinman, Scott Tennent, Jennifer Thompson, Paul G. Wagner, Joe Weston, and Deb Wood of Princeton Architectural Press
—Kevin Lippert, Publisher

LIBRARY OF CONGRESS
CATALOGING-IN-PUBLICATION DATA
Nash, Eric Peter.
Manhattan skyscrapers / Eric P. Nash ; photographs by Norman McGrath ; introduction by Carol Willis.—Rev. and expanded ed.
p. cm.
Includes bibliographical references.
ISBN 1-56898-545-2 (alk. paper)
1. Skyscrapers—New York (State)—New York. 2. Architecture—New York (State)—New York—20th century.
3. Manhattan (New York, N.Y.)—Buildings, structures, etc.
I. McGrath, Norman. II. Title.
NA6232.N37 2005
720'.483'097471—dc22
2005002264

Para Rebecca, rosa rara, perla preciosa, hija hermosa de la luna

Contents

Acknowledgments

A BOOK, like a skyscraper, is put together by many unseen hands. Thanks to my editors and draftsmen, Beth Harrison at Princeton Architectural Press and Julie Iovine at the *New York Times*, for their sharp minds and pencils, and general grace under pressure. My publisher, Kevin Lippert, provided the site to build upon. Norman McGrath created the framework of color photographs by which this sheath of text hangs. Eugenia Bell laid the foundation with intrepid archival photo research. Like a master mason, the design director Sara Stemen put the pieces in place. Sylvie Ball did the finish carpentry with several supplemental photographs, and the architectural historian John Kriskiewicz helped get the customers in the door with his insightful introduction. Carol Willis, the director of the Skyscraper Museum, deliriously transformed my view of the city when I learned in her class at the New School for Social Research that the Empire State Building's crown was designed as a mooring mast for zeppelins. And thanks to my sister, Laura, who has been as true as a surveyor's level in helping me set my sights.

Wow! New York, just like I pictured it . . . skyscrapers and everything!

—Stevie Wonder

. . . when I try to imagine a faultless love
Or the life to come, what I hear is the murmur
Of underground streams, what I see is a limestone landscape.

—W. H. Auden

CAROL WILLIS

SKYSCRAPER HISTORY changed on September 11, 2001. This book, first published in 1999, needs a new edition, if only to place the entry on the World Trade Center in the past tense and to acknowledge that the title is tinged with tragedy. Academics debate perspectives through which we view the past, and in the late twentieth century the postmodern mindset argued the impossibility of a single truth or unshifting narrative. But the first year of the twenty-first century proved that there are some historical markers that are definitive and indelible.

Exactly what has changed, though, is hard to pinpoint. "Our first skyscraper martyrs" is how critic Paul Goldberger described the loss of the twin towers and the emotional public response. New York's shared sorrow over the structures stands in striking contrast to sentiments in the last years of the twentieth century, when there was a clear animus in the city against tall buildings. Preservationists and good-government groups marshaled protests and lawsuits that stymied towers such as the early Columbus Circle project (now completed as the Time Warner Building), and the Department of City Planning sought to curtail height by revising the zoning code in an ultimately failed effort inelegantly, but aptly, named the Unified Bulk Proposal.

Post 9/11, there seems to have been a shift in both popular and critical perception: soaring height now seems to transcend the association of private interests and investment and represent a collective identity. There is a new emotional connection to the skyline. The fervent desire to fill the void at Ground Zero with a monumental tower has had overwhelming support, even if the design of the Freedom Tower has been controversial. Other bold tower proposals throughout the city by international celebrity architects have been eagerly embraced.

Lamenting lost landmarks is a tradition in writing about New York, especially since the 1960s, when the demolition of masterworks such as Pennsylvania Station spurred grassroots political efforts to create the Landmarks Preservation Commission. Books like Nathan Silver's classic *Lost New York* (1967) mourned the disappearance of the nineteenth-century architecture of the city—from individual mansions, to blocks of early row houses, to grand

civic and commercial structures of two to ten stories. *The Destruction of Lower Manhattan* (1969), an album by photographer Danny Lyons, captured the last remnants of downtown's working waterfront at the moment of massive urban renewal, including the construction of the new World Trade Center. In this storyline, skyscrapers were the ultimate villains in a march of modernity that squashed human scale and erased history.

It is a cliché that the essential characteristic of New York is continuous change. But a walk through the streets today—the dense urban fabric of lower Manhattan, the spine of Broadway as it travels up the island, the corporate corridor of Park Avenue, still mixed with patrician co-ops and Art Deco hotels—shows how rich and ranging an archive of American architecture remains in the city. In *Manhattan Skyscrapers*, we have a happy survey of survivors.

Eric Nash and Norman McGrath have selected a set of gems that span the 1890s to the present. From the early, eclectic American Tract Society Building and Louis H. Sullivan's refined Bayard-Condict Building, to the Park Row Building, the turn-of-the-century title holder for world's tallest building, through the classical monumentality of the Flatiron Building, Metropolitan Life Insurance Company Tower, and Bankers Trust Company Building and the Gothic spire of the Woolworth Building, we see the highlights of the first, laissez-faire era of skyscraper development, when no constraints tailored the foursquare form of these straight-up structures.

The second era was distinctively shaped by the setback formula of the 1916 zoning law, which produced the stepped-pyramid bases and slender tower shafts of the Art Deco stars of the 1920s and early 1930s, including the Chanin, Chrysler, General Electric, and Empire State buildings. These Jazz Age greats have an impressive backup band in midtown that each get a riff here. Downtown, a second scene hits the high notes with the Wall Street cluster of 40 Wall, One Wall, and City Bank Farmers Trust and Cities Service buildings. Clearly Nash's favorites, the 1920s towers dominate the book in number and personality, just as they seem to define New York in the mind's eye of millions or in the top-ten lists of tourists.

In the first half of the history of the New York skyscraper, steel frames were clad in stone, brick, or terra cotta and offered the illusion of monumental mass. In the second half, from the 1940s through today, the aesthetic has been principally transparent planes and volumes, a curtain wall that reveals the structural system and the space within. Advances in technology, including high-strength steel, bolted and welded skeletons, curtain-wall systems, air-conditioning, and fluorescent lights, made these innovations possible, and the triumph of International Style modernism made the glass box ubiquitous. McGrath has a special empathy for the modernist towers, shooting them for the most part either face-on or slightly angled to define their precise prismatic volumes. From the paragons of the style—Lever House, Seagram Building, and Black Rock (CBS Building), to the interchangeable tower-in-the-plaza slabs of Sixth Avenue and other like-minded monoliths—Nash and McGrath give Manhattan modernism due respect. Likewise, the buildings of the last decades of the century, which range from the slick surface of the Lipstick Building, the punning postmodern AT&T (Sony) Building, and the collaged façades of 4 Times Square, to the folded-glass envelopes of 1 and 2 UN Plaza and the faceted LVMH Building, are presented with flair, flash, and cool.

Still, *Manhattan Skyscrapers* has an everyday quality, in the best sense of the word. McGrath's photographs generally portray his subjects in full daylight (not the dramatic raking light of dawn or sunset or other types of atmospherics), and the towers are embedded in the city, as they are in life. These are the buildings, from masterpieces to mundane, that New Yorkers see around them every day. Nash's entries are minihistories that are sensitive, informative, and fun to read: they make the buildings approachable.

One thing we have learned from 9/11 is that the everyday architecture we take for granted is really something to treasure. The Twin Towers were giants the likes of which we will not see again. But contrary to the questions posed by so many journalists and writers in the months after the tragedy, it is clear that New York is going to keep building towers. *Manhattan Skyscrapers* will surely have another new edition.

Manhattan
Skyscrapers

American Tract Society Building

T WO COMPETING styles of architecture predominated in the United States when the American Tract Society Building was completed. The earlier style was Richardsonian Romanesque, named for Henry Hobson Richardson, critically considered to be our first native-born architect of world-class genius. Richardson combined the massive, lithic qualities of the Roman stone arch with his own uncanny sense of flowing, organic energy and balanced asymmetry. The other style, called Sullivanesque for Louis Henry Sullivan, represented a break with the past because it was an expression of the new tall building as a vertical design.

R. H. Robertson's 23-story American Tract Society Building is a premodern skyscraper in that its primary organization is horizontal. The arcaded, rock-faced granite ashlar base takes its inspiration from Florentine palazzi, an appropriate image for the expanding mercantile and industrial empire of the United States. The building was commissioned by the American Tract Society, which published Bibles in the interest of promoting a universal, nondenominational Protestantism, the culture of the emerging business class. Robertson was an ecclesiastical architect, familiar with the then-popular Romanesque style, so it was natural for him to design a Romanesque skyscraper.

Robertson made no attempt to unify the building vertically, as Sullivan would have done. The styling of the squarish tower on a 100-by-94-foot site is Renaissance, with stacked, horizontal layers separated by numerous beltcourses and window moldings. At 291 feet tall, the building was skyscraper height for its day (the world's record was still held by the 302-foot-tall Masonic Temple of 1892 by Burnham & Root in Chicago). However, its relatively low scale and proportions of 3:1 make the Renaissance styling visually appealing.

The three-story crown at the corner of Nassau and Spruce Streets adds visual interest by

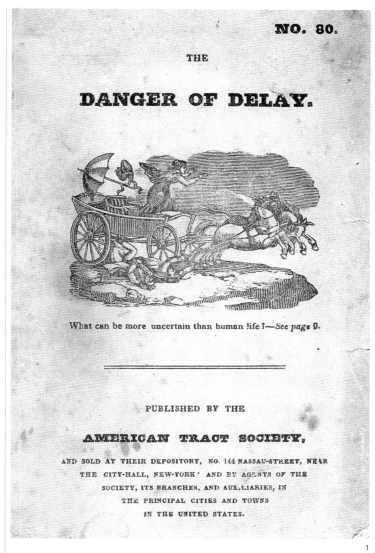

breaking up the roofline against the sky, an early eclectic forebear of the fanciful Art Deco crowns. A double-arcaded window with deep intrados is supported by a three-quarter-round brick Corinthian column and heavy scroll brackets. A curved copper cornice decorated with egg-and-dart molding and lion's heads surmounts the hollow double arches, and terracotta winged angel caryatids, an appropriate

motif for a Bible publisher, look out from the corners.

At the time, there was no consensus on how to treat the top of a tall building and all kinds of variations on historicist styles were attempted, from Gothic spires to Greek temples. These richly detailed sculptural cornices became obsolete when buildings regularly were 30 and 40 stories tall.

[1] A typical pamphlet published by the American Tract Society.

Bayard-Condict Building

65—69 BLEECKER STREET » LOUIS H. SULLIVAN, 1898

mullions. The regular, square-headed windows of the open, glassy façade visually recede into the background behind the organizing vertical lines of white terra cotta. The piers themselves are decorated with fluted piping that further enhances the vertical line.

The thin curtain wall of terra cotta that expresses the inner steel skeleton was a radical departure from the heavy masonry walls of the period. Montgomery Schuyler, a leading critic of the time, wrote of the Bayard, "Everywhere the drapery of baked clay is a mere wrapping, which clings so closely to the frame as to reveal it, and even to emphasize it.... The Bayard Building is the nearest approach yet made, in New York, at least, to solving the problem of the skyscraper."

Though known for saying "form ever follows function," Sullivan was a poet rather than a pure functionalist at heart. The six spread-winged angels at the cornice express the building's soaring aspirations, making it part of an oneiric cityscape.

LOUIS HENRY SULLIVAN'S graceful, terra-cotta-clad Bayard-Condict Building does not quite qualify as a skyscraper at only 13 stories, but Sullivan revolutionized the way architects think about tall buildings. As Frank Lloyd Wright told the story, Louis Sullivan invented the modern skyscraper after a walk through Chicago's Loop, when in three minutes he dashed off an esquisse for the Wainwright Building (1891) in St. Louis. "I was perfectly aware of what had happened," wrote Wright, who was then Sullivan's apprentice. "This was Louis Sullivan's greatest moment—his greatest effort. The 'skyscraper' as a new thing under the sun, an entity with . . . beauty all its own, was born."

Sullivan's contribution was nothing less than to overthrow the heritage of Greek and Roman architecture. Before the age of elevators and structural steel, buildings were low to the ground and the emphasis was on the horizontal line. Even when new technologies allowed architects to build vertically, they adhered to the horizontal "layer-cake" construction of the classical model. Rather than counteract the inherent verticality of a tall building by imposing a horizontal plan, Sullivan realized that a skyscraper "must be tall, every inch of it tall. . . . It must be every inch a proud and soaring thing, rising in sheer exaltation that from bottom to top it is a unit without a single dissenting line."

This commercial office building, the only example of Sullivan's work in New York, appears much taller than its neighbors because of its elegantly organized façade. The structural piers that run the entire length of the façade from the ground floor to the deep overhanging cornice are distinguished by their heft and thickness. In contrast, the three-quarter-round colonettes that serve as window mullions begin at the second floor, above open spaces, denoting their decorative rather than structural function.

Sullivan created a new visual lexicon for the tall building, in which everything is subordinated to the vertical expression. The surface of the spandrels is suppressed behind the piers and

[1] Richly ornamental terra-cotta panels incorporate classical and Celtic motifs.   [2] Breathtakingly modern, the Bayard dates to the horse-and-carriage era.

Park Row Building

THE VICTORIAN culture that produced the first skyscrapers was an odd mix of forward-looking technology and romantic nostalgia for the bucolic past that technology was replacing. The 30-story, 391-foot-tall Park Row Building, for nine years the world's tallest building, was constructed with an internal steel cage frame pioneered by the Chicago School, but its cluttered classical revival façade works to disguise its height rather than accentuate it.

R. H. Robertson drew on metaphors from an age before steel construction. Four massive limestone caryatids at the fourth-four level, sculpted by John Massey Rhind, emphasize an illusion of masonry support in the buff-brick and limestone façade, even though steel girders can be plainly seen bracing the light courts. The vertical organization of the building is confused by horizontal divisions of stringcourses and heavily bracketed balconies at many levels.

Robertson apparently could not decide between presenting the building as a free-standing tower or a simple infill. As a result, the building partakes of both and has virtually no distinguishing silhouette. The presentation is almost entirely oriented toward its 104-foot-wide Park Row façade, except for the narrow 20-foot-wide front on Ann Street to the south. Ells sprawl octopus-like, covered only by bare brick party walls.

Diminutive, copper-covered cupolas that once served as a public observatory are a wonderful romantic holdover, but also reveal a miscomprehension of the impact of classical decoration on a tall building. Seen from street level, the tiny turrets only work to lessen the scale of the building. The design problem of topping off a tall building led to eclectic and at times eccentric variations before the setback silhouette was arrived upon in response to the Zoning Code of 1916.

In 1890, less than a decade before the Park Row was completed, there were only six

buildings over 10 stories tall in New York; by 1908, when the title of world's tallest building was ceded to Ernest F. Flagg's 47-story, 612-foot-tall Singer Building, there were 538 buildings over 10 stories. The benchmark of 10 stories rapidly became meaningless in the explosion of commercial construction. An apostate, Robertson recanted the skyscraper aesthetic in 1900, and argued for a return to the Beaux-Arts scale, in which new buildings should be no higher than 150 feet on avenues (roughly the traditional cornice level of Park Avenue), and 100 feet on side streets.

The Park Row's lobby is a period gem, well worthy of landmark designation, although it is not one. Nearly perfectly preserved, it is lined with marble panels that would become the trademark of New York office buildings until well into the 1960s, under a gilded, coffered ceiling. Ten remarkable wedge-shaped elevator cabs fan out to form a semicircle.

Developed as a speculative commercial office venture by a syndicate of investors, the Park Row contained nearly 1,000 office spaces and accommodated 4,000 workers. It was emblematic of the gigantism to come. *Munsey's* magazine called it "a city and a world within four towering walls . . . a footprint of the twentieth century."

[1] The Park Row Building's semicircular lobby features wedge-shaped elevator cabs.   [2] The building's steel structure is belied by its masonry motifs.

Flatiron Building

175 FIFTH AVENUE » DANIEL H. BURNHAM, 1902

WELL PAST World War I, the steamship continued to be the most powerful metaphor for the twentieth century. Nautical design demanded that no space be wasted, no gesture be superfluous, and that an object's form be subordinated to its use. It is not coincidental that the Flatiron Building so much resembles a steamship fashioned out of stone. Alfred Stieglitz, who took one of the best-known images of the sheer, thin wall of the Flatiron floating weightlessly above the snow of Madison Square Park, wrote that the building "appeared to be moving toward me like the bow of a monster ocean steamer—a picture of new America still in the making." With its undulating French Renaissance terra-cotta cladding, the Flatiron seems to swim out of a dream of a classical past toward the future of the steel skyscraper. It is a perfect snapshot of the skyscraper as a Janus-faced evolutionary object, looking back to the past, but anticipating the future.

Originally built as the headquarters of the George A. Fuller construction company, the building was only briefly called the Fuller Building and soon became known as the Flatiron because of its distinctive shape. The company built some of the most important buildings in the city, including the original Pennsylvania Station, the Plaza Hotel, and Lever House and the Seagram Building in the post–World War II era. The 21-story, 307-foot-tall building was the tallest skyscraper north of Wall Street when it was built.

Buckminster Fuller rightly remarked that the Flatiron dated to an era when "architects were still pretending there was no steel," but the Chicago architectural firm of Daniel H. Burnham was already one step ahead. Burnham maximized the delta-shaped site to establish the skyscraper as a freestanding sculptural object, but the viewer intuits that the walls are too sheer to support its weight. The onlooker cannot help but be swept into the vortex of its six-foot-wide

1

apex at the intersection of Broadway and Fifth Avenue. The radically narrow corner seems to compress space, making the viewer look up for the lost volume of the building, further adding to a sense of overwhelming height.

Sometimes called "Burnham Baroque," the rippling terra-cotta curtain wall decorated with lion's heads, wreaths, and architectural masks is a link with a classical past. At the fourth story, foliated ovals alternate with roundels that contain mysterious Greek masks of women. The terra-cotta blocks are deeply incised and richly patterned, creating a florid play of light and shadow over the entire surface. The windows, set in deep reveals, seem like somber voids in the surface. Eight-story oriels, relatively rare in New

[1] The underlying steel skeleton stands exposed in this construction photo.

York office buildings but more common in Chicago skyscrapers such as Burnham's Fisher Building of 1896, give an undulating rhythm to the façade. The banded rustication of the walls enhances the sense of many layers stacked on top of one another.

The Flatiron is one of the most aggressive formulations of the tall building as a classical column, with a defined, anchoring base, a regular shaft, and an ornamental capital. The base, which can be read as four or five stories because of the double-height ground floor, is distinguished by heavily rusticated limestone blocks. Burnham capped his building with a massive, projecting dentiled cornice topped by flat balustrades interspersed with squat piers. The fact that from certain angles the building can be perceived as a column is a marvelously literal demonstration of the essence of the free-standing tower.

The column form was the summa for a skyscraper of this height, but at greater distances of 30 and 40 stories that tall buildings soon attained, heavy, classical cornices became unwieldy. Ely Jacques Kahn, one of the most prolific architects of the setback style, perhaps now remains alone in his judgment, but wrote: "Consider the Flatiron, the Tribune Tower, the World Building as notable shafts of a generation ago and find how little reason exists for most of their decoration and how feebly they stop. The cornice, once of stone and purporting to shed rain water from the face of the building, became a distorted and ridiculous affair of tin, copper, sheet iron, terra cotta, tied on with wires and merely lasting as a weak reminder of mere classicism."

But the Flatiron is a thoroughly modern object in that it requires the viewer to complete the picture. There is no single image of the building; it depends on your point of view. From head-on it is a flying wedge; from close up it is a dizzying wall that seems to have no more depth than a standing column; and from broadside, the 190-foot-wide façade on Broadway presents a palazzo of almost unimaginable scale. The wall is as massive yet knifelike as the prow of a ship. The image is not stable, resonating between stasis and motion, giving a sense of dynamism to the whole that predicted the restless forward momentum of the twentieth century.

[1] The Flatiron's dynamic apex appears to be a pure column.   [2] From uptown. the Flatiron looks like either a sheer. six-foot-thick wall. or a steamship prow.

West Street Building

(now 90 West Street)

CASS GILBERT, 1907

THE WEST STREET BUILDING is a Gilded Age skyscraper, a celebration of wealth and culture in terra cotta, but also incorporates some of the most forward-looking ideas in skyscraper design. From Louis Sullivan, Cass Gilbert took the idea of clearly expressing the underlying steel structure: broad piers that support the West Street Building rise without interruption from street level to an arcaded crown, while decorative, three-quarter-round colonettes run only the length of the shaft. The shaft's overall verticality is emphasized by its simple lines and recessed spandrels. Rows of windows between the piers form nearly uninterrupted perpendicular strips of glazing, adding to the airiness and openness of the façade.

Following Burnham, Gilbert treated the tall building as a classical column, with a three-story limestone base, Gothic ornamentation, unaccented modernistic shaft, and crown that resembles a fireworks explosion in terra cotta. In an advance in skyscraper design, the West Street Building presents its crown rather than the detailing of the whole façade as the image of the building. In his Woolworth Building six years later, Gilbert took this idea a step further by making the silhouette the overall symbol of the skyscraper. With a sculptor's sense for visual progression, Gilbert leads the eye up from the West Street Building's massive white granite base, through the sweeping verticals of the matching white terra-cotta shaft to the six-story crown, where the gaze becomes lost in a cannonade of French and Belgian Gothic detail. Red granite columns flanking the entrances, windows framed in green cast iron, and the lushly tinted, overscale, polychrome terra-cotta rosettes in the intrados of the arches play vibrantly against the building's stark white skin. The eye devours the surface, seeking a resting point, traveling up the blank piers only to be brought earthward again by the grand three-story arches in the capital, then returning upward to seek out the finer details of corbels, turrets, dormers, and pinnacles in the crown. The festive composition is framed by the rigorously simple roofline and heavy corner piers, a great visual balancing act between the tension of curved and straight lines.

Set around a rear light court, the U-shaped building is now hemmed in by the superscale One World Trade Center just across narrow Liberty Street, but originally commanded a more prominent site at what was then the edge of the Hudson River. The first occupants were members of the proliferating railroad and ferry industries. Cesar Pelli paid a contextual tribute to this festive holdover from the ancien régime by echoing the West Street Building in the decorative glass mastaba crown of his No. 1 World Financial Center.

[1] Illuminated at night, the West Street's attic is a monument to the Gilded Age.   [2] The West Street Building dominated the Hudson River waterfront before the landfill.   [3] A relatively plain base and shaft lead up to the crown's visual pyrotechnics.

Metropolitan Life Insurance Company Tower

ONE MADISON AVENUE » NAPOLEON LEBRUN & SONS, 1909

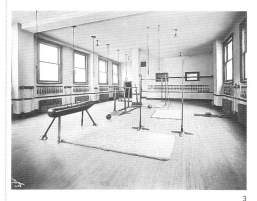

ITHOUT A clear precedent for what the world's tallest building should look like, Pierre L. LeBrun of Napoleon LeBrun & Sons reached back to one of the best-known buildings in history—the campanile of St. Mark's in Venice—for his model. The scale problems of transposing an historical style to a skyscraper are immediately apparent: stretching 700 feet, one inch, from the sidewalk, the Met Life Tower does not seem particularly tall or distinctive.

In the American race to outdo all the records of the Old World, at least in sheer size, the Met Life Tower is more than twice the height of the original 325-foot-tall Campanile. The Met Life's proportions are that of a Doric column applied to a 52-story building. The shaft is organized into three bays of three windows each, bracketed by rusticated quoins, ending in an arcaded loggia at the thirty-first floor. However, the height of the new tower is coun-

teracted, because the mind's eye inevitably shrinks it back down to the scale of sixteenth-century Venice.

Ornamentation was not meant to be viewed so far from the ground. The four-sided, 26.5-foot-in-diameter clock faces with four-foot-tall numerals and minute hands weighing half a ton lose their impact at such distances. The high pyramidal roof with ocular windows is topped with a cupola and glazed lantern that was lit at night. Dolphin's head balustrades and lion's heads once adorned the now-severe lines of the shaft. The tower, originally sheathed in Tuckahoe marble, was stripped in a 1964 renovation and recovered in plain limestone. However, the architect's drawing is still preserved inside a 14.5-foot-tall frame at the 320 Park Avenue entrance. The simple fact of skyscraper design, that details had to be outscaled to be perceived at all, may have contributed as much to the spare, modernist style as much as any structural considerations. The building's massing and its

overall silhouette become more critical to its appearance at great distances than the façade detailing.

Experimenting with eclectic styles continued into the late 1950s, culminating in the Neo-Renaissance crown of 40 Wall Street, which Philip Johnson recently admired as "among New York's prettiest towers." LeBrun was less confident about the future of the skyscraper: "Whether architects are working toward the right evolution of a tall building, irreverently termed 'skyscraper design,' the verdict of time only can determine."

[1] Met Life executives prepare to drive in the ceremonial last rivet in 1908. [2] The Metropolitan Life Tower's familiar outline fights the impact of its height. [3] The executive gym, complete with medicine balls and Indian clubs.

Bankers Trust Company Building

(originally 14 Wall Street)   14–16 WALL STREET » TROWBRIDGE & LIVINGSTON, 1912

THE PERVADING metaphor for the skyscraper in the eclectic era was monumentality. As a powerful but young nation, America felt a need to compete with the landmarks of history. If not in age, we could outdo the past in sheer size and height: The Met Life Tower was twice as big as the original in Venice; the Woolworth outdid London's Houses of Parliament and the cathedrals of Europe as the world's tallest building. Trowbridge & Livingston turned to one of the best known images from antiquity—the pyramidal Mausoleum at Halicarnassus (c. 352 B.C.)—to cap off their 37-story skyscraper at the corner of Wall and Nassau Streets. At 539 feet tall, but with fronts measuring only 94 by 97 feet, it was considered the world's tallest structure on so small a site.

The formidable four-story granite base, sited on one of the most valuable intersections in the world at the corner of Wall and Nassau Streets, is patterned like a colonnade atop a classical stylobate. Three-story-tall, three-quarter-round Ionic columns marching across the façade above Greek fretwork are interrupted by garlanded beltcourses, and support an echinated, dentiled cornice decorated with rosettes and lion's heads.

Above the highly decorative base, derived from the Erectheum Ionic order, the plain, curtain-walled shaft that houses office rental space rises for 20 stories. The light gray granite façades of the square tower are organized into five bays of two windows, with little decoration other than the flat voussoirs surmounting the windows. Deep reveals give an impression of lithic solidity.

In a strange synchronicity, the crown seems to anticipate the jagged figure-ground effects of the later setback style. The granite-clad pyramid, which housed record rooms and storage space, caught the public's eye, and soon was claimed as the registered trademark for the bank. The pyramid top is also one of the most influential

3

designs on other downtown skyscrapers, repeated in the 480-foot-high Standard Oil Building (Carrère & Hastings and Shreve, Lamb & Blake, 1922) and Kevin Roche John Dinkeloo, & Associates' glassy postmodern Morgan Bank Headquarters (1988) at 60 Wall Street.

The Bankers Trust Company was founded to provide fiduciary services in cooperation rather than competition with commercial banks. The mighty enterprises of capitalism are symbolized in the bronze gate inside the lobby, which was renovated in 1931–33: a tipping vat of molten ore represents metallurgy; a helm interlaced with rigging stands for shipping; a derrick ball and rivets stand for construction; a generator with zigzag lightning bolts that anticipates Expressionist motifs stands for power; and an ox-head, engine valves, and shovel-head with paired sticks of dynamite represent agriculture, manufacturing, and mining, respectively.

[1] The pyramidal top is one of the most influential designs on downtown skyscrapers.

Woolworth Building

233 BROADWAY » CASS GILBERT, 1913

The Woolworth rises from a 29-story platform to become a tower inset on all four sides at the forty-second story. Like a medieval spire, the tower metamorphoses from a square to an octagon at the forty-eighth story, and culminates in a three-story, 125-foot-tall, copper-clad roof. The Woolworth stands out among its contemporaries because Gilbert resolved the problem of placing a smaller tower on top of a base by integrating the tower into the front façade. The building was designed to be seen as a free-standing tower, so all four sides were treated architecturally.

The three-story limestone base with granite at street level is topped by creamy, ivory-colored terra-cotta cladding anchored to a brick backing. Terra cotta, a light and decorative—rather than structural—material, emphasizes the steel cage that supports the building. The straight, structural lines of the piers end in the tower decorated with gargoyles, turrets, pinnacles, buttresses, and delicately colored terra-cotta panels in shades of green, cobalt blue, sienna, and deep rose. Gilbert skillfully used polychromy to bring out the relief of the façade.

The Woolworth was the era's most prominent example of the confluence of advertising and ego that went into skyscraper development. Frank Winfield Woolworth, the founder of the Woolworth retail chain, specifically instructed

SKYSCRAPERS ARE not only objects of their own time, but have an uncanny knack for pointing the way to the future. Cass Gilbert's Woolworth Building is the most successfully realized skyscraper of the eclectic era, but also seems to anticipate the setback designs of the Art Deco skyscrapers. At 55 stories, the Woolworth was the tallest and most recognizable skyscraper in the world for 16 years until it was topped by the Chrysler Building. Many heights are given for the building, but its highest point is 793.5 feet on the Barclay Street side. The owner had the building measured himself to make sure it was the tallest in the world. The stories that vary from 11 to 20 feet high are the equivalent of about 80 modern-day stories.

Gilbert decided on the Flamboyant Gothic style of fifteenth-century France to express the

building's height because he liked the visual interest of the style's summits. The skyscraper, he wrote, "is a monument whose masses must become more and more inspired the higher it rises. The Gothic style gave us the possibility of expressing the greatest degree of aspiration . . . the ultimate note of the mass gradually gaining in spirituality the higher it mounts."

The building soon became known as the "Cathedral of Commerce," a designation that Gilbert bristled at, because the sources of his inspiration had all been secular northern Gothic structures. The Gothic style influenced early skyscraper architects because it was the only historicist style that emphasized height and verticality. The tallest manmade point in Manhattan for more than half a century was the 284-foot steeple of Trinity Church, designed by Richard Upjohn in 1846.

[1] The world's tallest building at the time pierces the clouds.

[2] A 1910 study for the Woolworth; the owner rejected many early versions.

his architect to "make it 50 feet taller than the Metropolitan Tower," so that his new building would beat the record. Woolworth recognized the symbolic and advertising function of the world's tallest building: "I do not want a mere building," he said after revising dozens of Gilbert's sketches. "I want something that will be an ornament to the city."

Gilbert felt to a large degree that his design was simply a logical expression of the demands of the project, as did William Lamb with the Empire State Building. "The economic conditions which call for the use of every bit of available space and at the same time provide ample light for rooms leave little opportunity for the arrangement of the masses," Gilbert said. Nonetheless, the Woolworth abounds with details that transcend the merely functional. The lobby is ahistorically designed in a Romanesque style featuring barrel-vaulted ceilings with glass mosaics patterned after the early Christian mausoleum Galla Placidia in Ravenna, Italy. The polished steel doors with gold backgrounds at street level were produced by the Tiffany Studios, and the walls are lined with dark, fine-veined marble from the Greek island of Skyros.

The extraordinary corbel grotesques in the lobby form a parable of how a skyscraper is financed and constructed. There is the developer, the mustachioed Frank Woolworth, counting out the coins of his five-and-ten-cent fortune. (Woolworth actually paid the $13.5 million construction costs in cash as the building proceeded, so that it opened without a mortgage or debt of any kind.) A bespectacled Cass Gilbert cradles a scale model of his setback tower, and the structural engineer, Gunwald Aus, who also worked on Gilbert's West Street Building, measures a steel girder. Louis J. Horowitz, head of the Thompson-Starrett Building Company, lambastes a contractor over the telephone, and Edward J. Hogan, the rental agent, peruses a lease.

4

[1] F. W. Woolworth counts out his five-and-dime fortune in a corbel caricature.   [2] The builder, in a monk's hood, talks into a stand-up telephone.   [3] The Woolworth's terra-cotta cladding accentuates the underlying steel structure.
[4] The tower's electrifying modernistic impact is often overlooked because of its Gothic styling.

Municipal Building

CENTRE STREET AT CHAMBERS STREET » MCKIM, MEAD & WHITE, 1914

THE MUNICIPAL BUILDING was the first skyscraper constructed by McKim, Mead & White, in the waning years of the firm's influential Beaux-Arts career. The 40-story building, which contains 650,000 square feet of city offices, was designed by the partner William Mitchell Kendall. Charles McKim himself was averse to skyscrapers and the trend towards gigantism and said, "I think the skyline of New York daily grows more hideous." The Municipal Building features some of the best aspects of Beaux-Arts architecture, which sought to be both monumental and an integral part of the city's fabric. The 559-foot-tall building, including a 15-story tower, is superbly metropolitan: it straddles the extension of Chambers Street (now closed to traffic) with a Roman triumphal arch like a modern-day Colossus of Rhodes. The 24-story wings of the U-shaped court, covered in light-colored Maine granite, reach out to embrace City Hall.

The Municipal Building is both ceremonial and sheltering. Adolph A. Weinman's 20-foot-high gilded statue of "Civic Fame," the largest statue in the city, holds aloft a crown with five turrets, symbolizing the five boroughs of New York City. A giant Corinthian colonnade, modeled after Giovanni Lorenzo Bernini's colonnade at St. Peter's, marches across the entrance, a protective yet penetrable perimeter. Vaults of Guastavino tile protect commuters in a loggia on the south concourse of the subway. Although the Woolworth Building was the first to provide sheltered subway entrances from the sidewalks of the side streets, the Municipal Building was the first to incorporate a subway station as an integral part of its base.

Henry Hope Reed exulted that the Municipal Building was "the nation's finest skyscraper," but here we see the Beaux-Arts style stretching at the seams to cope with the new demand for height. The insistent horizontal styling of classical architecture fights with the sense of height, so that the building appears more like a massive wall with a tower, rather than a tall building.

The crown of a Corinthian drum adapted from the Choregic Monument of Lysicrates in Athens of 334 B.C. is a kind of funerary monument for historical styles. There were simply too few models left to copy, and skyscraper design had to move forward instead of back. A comparison with developments in the other arts is telling: in 1913, the Armory Show featured new works by Picasso, Braque, and Duchamp, and James Joyce published *Dubliners*.

However, the building's Imperial Roman image was enormously influential in other cities, and was a prototype for Chicago's Wrigley Building (1924) and Cleveland's Terminal Tower (1930), both by Graham, Anderson, Probst & White; the Fisher Building in Detroit (Albert Kahn, 1928); and—strangely enough at such a late date—the main building of Moscow University (L. V. Rudnev, S. E. Chernyshov, P. V. Abrosimov, and A. F. Khryakov, 1949–53). The Municipal Building houses a Dickensian maze of old-fashioned city offices, and dozens of couples still marry here every week.

[1] The gold-leafed statue of "Civic Fame" atop the Municipal Building.   [2] The Municipal Building, near completion in 1912, is a monument to civic pride.

Candler Building

220 WEST 42ND STREET » WILLAUER, SHAPE & BREADY, 1914

THE PROTO-SETBACK silhouette of the Candler Building seems to summon the future in a dream form, with its embryonic winged base, its plain, functional shaft, and its indented crown. The Candler sets an important precedent, because it was one of the most successful solutions to the problem of building on a midblock site. The architects solved the problem of how to make a tower stand out among lower flanking buildings by setting it off on its own base, a model that neatly adapted itself to the requirements of the setback zoning code of 1916. Because of this organization, the outlines of the Candler predominate over its surface ornament.

Neglected by the public and critics alike for much of its 75-year history, the 24-story Candler Building, clad in gleaming white terra cotta, has become a showpiece of the recent Times Square revival. The Candler is a fascinating transitional form between the fussiness of classical revival skyscraper design and the emerging spare lines of modernism. Nominally Spanish Renaissance, the design is more important because the configuration of base, shaft, and crown anticipates the silhouette of the setback skyscraper.

Built as the New York headquarters of the Coca-Cola Company, and named after its founder Asa Candler, the tower rises from a five-story, 78-foot-wide arcaded base attached to the main shaft by unusual wings that give it the appearance of a finned 1950s rocket ship. Above the decorative fourth-floor spandrels, the shaft rises in three uninterrupted bays of metal-framed double windows for 13 stories, ending in arches that echo the base. The lines of the shaft are remarkably clean cut, without the stringcourses, colonettes, and gewgaws of its predecessors.

The crown above the projecting twentieth-floor cornice is not fully setback as later buildings would be, but is massed with corner indentations so that it is perceived as a separate section, surmounted by a pyramidal copper roof

1

352 feet above street level with a 36-foot flagpole. The Candler was the tallest building north of the Metropolitan Life Tower at 24th Street, and represented Manhattan's inexorable march uptown.

Much of the terra-cotta detailing of cherub's heads, architectural masks set in roundels, and well-articulated diapering is almost invisible from street level. A perforated railing of addorsed, overscaled sea horses and winged griffins at the top cornice compensates for the distance. This kind of ornamentation might cause one to speculate that American businessmen were furnishing an empyrean realm meant only for each other.

[1] Both of the base's embryonic "wings" are intact in this early photo.

Equitable Building

120 BROADWAY » ERNEST R. GRAHAM, 1915

THOUGH FREQUENTLY singled out as the behemoth that brought about the 1916 Zoning Code, the Equitable Building was still on the drawing boards when city planners were looking for ways to increase the amount of sunlight and air circulation to the streets. You need only stand on Pine Street to understand the problem: the sky is reduced to a narrow stretch of ribbon between the cornice of the 41-story Equitable and the 19-story 100 Broadway, less than 35 feet apart. The Equitable rises, cliff-like, straight from the sidewalk for 542 feet. The experience is like standing at the bottom of a man-made canyon. Even at noon in midsummer, the streets are half-plunged in shadow.

Before the advent of fluorescent office lighting, what most determined the value of office space (after location) was the amount of natural light it received. When the Equitable went up in 1915, it cast a shadow for four blocks uptown, causing surrounding real-estate values to plummet. Falling real-estate values meant falling tax assessments, and the city required a remedy, so that market logic as much as environmental concerns led to the zoning reform, the first of its kind in the nation. The timing of the 1916 Zoning Code was fortuitous, because architects working in eclectic styles were running out of ideas about how to treat the tall building. The code forced architects to think about skyscrapers in fresh ways.

Henry James meant buildings like the Equitable when he called skyscrapers "giants of the mere market." The Equitable packs in an astonishing 1.2 million square feet of rental space, or 30 times the area of its site, which is slightly less than an acre. The barrel-vaulted, block-long arcade of stores in the lobby was innovative, but its colossal scale, the ceiling studded with giant plaster rosettes, and the icy corridor lined in lustrous marble make you feel mouse-sized even today.

The Equitable was unpopular because of its banality as well as its bulk. Its unornamented 23-story shaft rises through sheer numbing repetition of layers of square-headed windows separated by piers of shallow pilasters. A course of undersized lion's heads at the twenty-fourth-story cornice seems to be an afterthought. The setback silhouette combined with the zigzag geometry of the 1925 Exposition Internationale des Arts Décoratifs et Industriels Modernes in Paris led to the astonishing richness of visual design in skyscrapers of the 1920s, a match made in the heavens.

[1] The Equitable rises through sheer multiplication of its one-acre site. [2] The steel skeleton of the Equitable Building tops out in August 1914. [3] The H-shaped Equitable stands out in bright contrast to the shadows of Lower Manhattan.

Bush Tower

THE NARROW 32-story Bush Tower was the first skyscraper built after the Zoning Code of 1916, but it had been designed before the code went into effect. Nonetheless, Harvey Wiley Corbett accurately foresaw how architects would respond to the new setback envelope presented by the code.

Like the Candler Building one block to the west, Bush Tower's most expressive feature is its lines rather than its surface ornament. Corbett clearly chose the English Gothic style for its emphasis on vertical lines. Much of the building's impact is due to its exiguous siting, with a 480-foot-tall sheer tower on a front only 50 feet wide and 90 feet deep. The decoration of the base and shaft is remarkably stripped down, confined to four limestone corbel gargoyles at street level that caricature the Bush Terminal Company's role in the shipping industry. The gargoyles depict a navigator with his sextant, a hardy helmsman wearing a sou'wester, a frightened cabin boy holding on to the mast, and a strangely apathetic sailor entangled with an anchor. Flush with the World War I effort, the Bush shipping and warehousing concern at one time occupied 150 buildings and eight piers on the west side of midtown.

Projecting triangular buff-brick mullions subdivide three deeply incised window bays. From an oblique angle, the reveals are so deep that the spandrels disappear entirely, giving the impression of a façade composed entirely of skinny vertical lines. John Mead Howells adapted this method of scraping lines into the façade to add verticality to his Beekman Tower in 1928.

A kind of proto-setback is formed at the twenty-fourth-story cornice line, where a six-story section is chamfered and set off by copper pinnacles at the four corners. Above the double-height top floor with pointed arch windows, a shallow mansard disguises a water tower. Corbett moved his offices into the top floor to watch his prophecies for the development of 42nd Street come true.

Corbett was clear about his plans for Bush Tower: "We were determined it should be a thing complete in itself, with fine, clean, uprising lines; a building that could be looked at from every angle, sides and back as well as front." In a brilliant design stroke, the Gothic styling of the party walls becomes a purely two-dimensional representation. In monochromatic brick, Corbett limned white piers that seem to cast a black "shadow," continuing the insistent verticality of the façade. On the eastern party wall, an overscaled pointed arch spanning the light court adds an upward-thrusting visual impact to what would have otherwise been a strictly utilitarian feature. The building is often photographed from this angle rather than from the main façade.

The symbolic Gothic trimming was an economical way of resolving the problem of whether the building would be perceived as a tower or piece of infill. At the same time, it was a statement by Corbett that the eclectic era's literal interpretation of historical styling was no longer necessary and that architects were free to use only what they needed from the past to create the future.

[1] Corbett watched the development of 42nd Street from his top-floor office.   [2] In 1927 Bush Tower signified the business district's shift to midtown.

Shelton Towers Hotel

(now Marriott East Side Hotel)   525 LEXINGTON AVENUE » ARTHUR LOOMIS HARMON, 1924

WITH THE Shelton Towers Hotel, the first tall building specifically designed to conform to the setback code, the skyscraper comes into its own as a symbol of modernism. The role of the Shelton's two most famous occupants—the painter Georgia O'Keeffe and her photographer husband Alfred Stieglitz—cannot be discounted in this process. The couple moved into a tiny, two-room apartment on the twenty-eighth floor with views of the East River shortly after their marriage in 1924.

Arthur Loomis Harmon was the first architect to exploit the aesthetic possibilities of the new zoning code envelope. Warren & Wetmore's 23-story Heckscher Building (1921, now the Crown) was actually the first skyscraper built after the code, but was really a 14-story classical revival tower with three-story wings set on a broad nine-story platform rather than a true setback. Harmon later joined Shreve &

Lamb to design the archetypal skyscraper, the Empire State Building.

Architects turned to ever more recondite sources from history and prehistory to fill the demand for buildings that met the code. Harmon adapted the massively lithic Lombard revival style of the Church of Sant'Ambrogio in Milan. His design is particularly successful because it relies on the overall grouping of large masses to form the building's image rather than ornamentation.

The warm, yellow-brick façade of the 32-story Shelton is treated as a single surface, so that the eye is drawn to the sculptural outlines of the cornices and setbacks. The tripartite grouping, set on a corner site, seems taller than it is because of a few tricks of classical masonry. The two-story limestone base slopes away from the viewer at street level, counteracting the sense that the building looms overhead. Upper stories employ entasis, the method of adding a slight bulge to long vertical elements so that they do

not appear to sag. Projecting brick headers add a texture of shadows. Shallow projecting 14-story bays form lights courts on three sides, around a central shaft that sets back at the twentieth-story cornice. Structural girders span a deep rear light court, but the building is meant to be perceived from all sides as a tower. The crown continues for an additional 10 stories, ending in a double arcade at the thirty-second floor. Griffins sejant face outward at the four corners. The surface is highly variegated, with the reveals of the piers standing out at different thicknesses. In directional light, the piers cast deep perpendicular lines of shadow that lend the building a sense of tapering height.

Except for its delightful limestone gargoyles, the Shelton is relatively free of ornamentation. Blind corbeled arcades line the cornice divisions, topped by a double-story crown under a mansard roof. The carved capitals of the three-story-tall columns at the base denote the Shelton's origins as an athletic club for men. One figure in a toga is ready to serve up a tennis ball, and another towels off after a swim.

Stieglitz and O'Keeffe were enormously fond of their nest in the sky. He took photographs of the raw new steel structures in midtown such as the Waldorf-Astoria. O'Keeffe painted abstracts of industrial views of the East River far below, and employed photographic techniques, such as the flare created by direct light in a camera lens, to paint *The Shelton with Sunspots*.

[1] Fanciful gargoyles and capitals adorn the base of this modernist milestone.

American Radiator Building

ACH MAJOR work in Raymond Hood's compressed, prolific career—cut short by his death at 53—is a fascinating metamorphosis from the skyscraper's Gothic roots to his early championship of the International Style in America. Hood and his collaborator John Mead Howell's winning entry for the highly visible Chicago Tribune Building competition in 1922 was a 36-story, 460-foot-tall version of Rouen Cathedral's Butter Tower in France, complete with eight overscaled flying buttresses. Sensitive to criticism that Eliel Saarinen's stripped-down, "styleless" (read modern) second-place entry was the superior design, Hood combined Gothic and modern styles in his American Radiator Building (though designed after the Tribune Building, the Radiator was actually completed a year earlier).

The Art Deco towers of midtown Manhattan were built within about a decade of one another and are textbook examples of how buildings learn from each other through synthesis. For his 22-story tower on a midblock site, Hood used the Candler's device of setting off the tower on a platform so that it would be freestanding. The Gothic style, stripped down to its symbolic essentials, is indebted to Corbett's Bush Tower. At the same time, Hood incorporated the clean, modernist lines of Saarinen's Tribune entry.

The Radiator is pivotal in the development of the skyscraper because it is the first true

2

3

expression of the Art Deco skyscraper silhouette. You can almost see the struggle to arrive at the form. From a complicated series of shallow setbacks at the sixteenth- and twentieth-story cornices, the distinctive step-like profile of the Art Deco skyscraper springs forth breathtakingly against the sky at the twenty-first floor. After the Radiator Building, architects would deal with the arrangement of large masses as solids set against the void of the sky. Hood intuitively understood this break with the past, and colored his building with black brick to emphasize that it should be perceived as a single, massive form. Usually, fenestration appears as darker holes in a light-colored building; here Hood makes the windows blend into the façade. The shaft's sculptural mass is intensified by the chamfered corners, which make the eye read it as a

continuous, wrapped surface. Gold-colored stone highlights the shifts in the setbacks.

The building's image was dramatically reversed at night, when glowing windows burned in the black façade and the crown was lit up, an attention-getting metaphor for the headquarters of a company that specialized in home heating. Playful, classically styled corbel figures at the third-story cornice, including a pipe fitter with a wrench, refer to great moments in the history of steam heat.

1

[1] Barrel-vaulted arches led to the showroom floor.   [2] Georgia O'Keeffe celebrated the tower in RADIATOR BUILDING AT NIGHT—NEW YORK, 1927.   [3] The pilaster bases reiterate the setback motif in miniature.

Ritz Tower

109 EAST 57TH STREET AT PARK AVENUE » EMERY ROTH AND CARRÈRE & HASTINGS, 1925

THE 546-FOOT tall, 41-story Ritz Tower, now lost in a shuffle of midsize buildings, was the first residential sky-scraper in the world. Emery Roth, whose main concern was to provide the comforts of Park Avenue living to its residents, seems to have done everything in his power to disguise the building's height. The resulting parfait is easy to find fault with: heavy, classical revival layers alternate with a few starkly bare stretchers thrown in for height. The Ritz is exactly the kind of building Ayn Rand scorned in her dizzy paean to the skyscraper, *The Fountainhead*, that "looked like a Renaissance palace made of rubber and stretched to the height of forty stories."

In an unpublished autobiography quoted in Steven Ruttenbaum's *Mansions in the Clouds: The Skyscraper Palazzi of Emery Roth*, the architect admitted, "It took years for me to forsake my early love and to forget Renaissance palaces and Greek and Roman temples." In the Ritz, Roth was trying to accomplish the contradictory goal of making the brand-new skyscraper form seem homey and familiar. He brought in Thomas Hastings, the surviving member of the great Beaux-Arts team of Carrère & Hastings, to decorate the façade with Italian Renaissance designs typical of Park Avenue's palazzo-like apartment buildings. Bronze-trimmed coach lanterns at the street level of the three-story rusticated limestone base welcome home the residents, and raised panels of putti and a winged cherub's head over the entrance symbolize home and family.

Roth seemed embarrassed about the vertical elements of the building, which emerge nakedly, like the limbs of an adolescent undergoing a growth spurt. No attempt was made to integrate the plain, unaccented, buff-brick shafts of square-headed windows with the ponderous balustrades, obelisks, cartouches, and broken pediments. The overall image of the building is a classical obelisk, but the form seems to stutter at every cornice, afraid to let the setbacks spring free. The crown, with its superfluous attic story under a mansard roof and heavy capping obelisk that recapitulates the overall parti looks as if it is trying to put a lid on the building's unseemly height.

New Yorkers, however, took to skyscraper living like ducks to the Lake in Central Park. The new status symbol was no longer a brownstone on a quiet side street, but a room with a view. The duplexes in the tower offered double-height, 40-foot-long living rooms with uninterrupted 25-mile views in all directions. The Ritz is an interesting transition from the cluttered comforts of the Edwardian era to the emerging slim lines of the Jazz Age. Roth achieved a more satisfying synthesis of styles in later designs for twin towers such as the San Remo and El Dorado apartment buildings, which look as if they have always belonged along Central Park West's skyline.

[1] The Ritz's Renaissance base abounds with symbols of domesticity.　[2] The Ritz is a giant obelisk, decorated with smaller obelisks.

Paramount Building

1501 BROADWAY » RAPP & RAPP, 1926

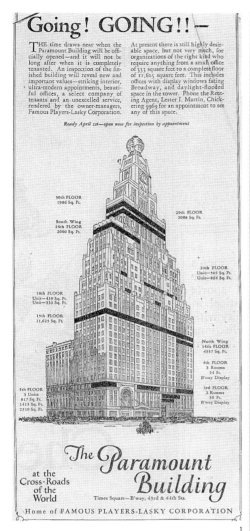

[1] A 1926 ad for the Paramount promotes "daylight-flooded space in the tower." **[2]** The fabled Paramount Theater's entrance and marquee are visible at left.

BY THE mid-1920s, architects were no longer trying to disguise their buildings under layers of classical design, but instead were looking for new ways to show off the setback style. Rapp & Rapp wanted to display a form that had never been seen before, at least outside of Mesoamerica. Their 33-story ziggurat in Times Square, then the tallest building on Broadway north of the Woolworth Building, is a fascinating transition from classical revival to Art Deco styling.

Best known for their opulent, Neo-Baroque movie palaces, Rapp & Rapp designed the crown of Paramount Picture's East Coast headquarters for maximum show-biz impact. Eight pyramidal buff-brick setbacks, capped by squat limestone obelisks, cascade down from a clock tower surmounted by a 19-foot-in-diameter glass globe, illuminated from within. The setback below the clock faces is flanked by three-story-tall scrolls, making the whole look like an overscaled desk clock. At night, the setbacks were spotlit to form the classic wedding-cake tiers of a New York skyscraper floating above Broadway.

Art Deco and classical revival styles are not fully integrated in the Paramount. The presentation of the jazzy crown is almost entirely frontal, so that from side angles it seems top heavy and almost two-dimensional, like a theatrical prop rather than an essential design element. The classical detailing of cartouches and low-relief scrollwork in the crown are smooth and blank, almost vestigial, as if on their way to extinction. In contrast, the street level is completely classical revival in flavor, from the exterior sheath of black granite to the plaster rosettes in the smallish, barrel-vaulted lobby. The Paramount represents the dual persona of an office building in an entertainment capital: a sobersided workplace in the daytime, and an illuminated fantasyland by night.

The ornamentation reflects the glamour of the movie business. The globe symbolizes Paramount's worldwide interests, and the power of its medium—light. The glowing, 25-foot-in-diameter clock faces feature five-pointed stars, which surround the mountain peak in the Paramount logo. It is not too much of a stretch to associate the mountain-like massing of Mayan architecture with the Paramount peak. The lively arts motif is carried through at street level, where bronze relief masks of Comedy and Tragedy are placed above the entrance, and bronze panels above the elevators show classical figures playing harps and bagpipes.

The illuminated, bowed canopy of the legendary Paramount Theater, where bobby-soxers swooned for Frank Sinatra, once stood on Broadway near the corner of West 43rd Street. The 10-story, triple-balconied space, where every major act from Benny Goodman to Buddy Holly played, was gutted in a renovation in the early 1960s to make offices, but the entrance is still marked by two bays of filled-in windows at the top of the four-story limestone base. The glass globe was restored in 1998, and plans are afoot to install a replica of the old theater marquee.

Barclay-Vesey Building

WHILE MOST architects in the late 1920s sported ever more fanciful crowns on their buildings—like bonnets in an Easter parade—Ralph Walker was more interested in the 1916 Zoning Code's effect on a building's overall massing. The outcome was the truest fulfillment of the skyscraper theorist Hugh Ferriss's febrile visions of buildings as "mountain-like masses." Le Corbusier liked the Barclay-Vesey's treatment of surface, mass, and volume so much that he made it the frontispiece of his seminal book *Towards a New Architecture* (1931).

The requirements for the 31-story tower were unusual: it occupies an entire rhomboid-shaped block, and was built to accommodate office space for 6,000 workers and to be a center of long-distance telephone switching equipment. As a result, the 52,000-square-foot base was much deeper than other buildings of the time, because there was less need for natural lighting.

A square, 18-story tower is pivoted in relation to the 11-story platform, which gives a corkscrew tension to the whole composition. The viewer is constantly presented with two conflicting images of the building: an oblique-angled, lithic mass, and a flat, steel-supported façade with acute angles as sharp as paper creases. From the West Street front, the 17-story wings, angled along the baseline, seem shallow and precipitous, but this is belied by the cavernous depth of the light court. The massively arcaded Moorish-style pedestrian loggia that penetrates the thin Washington Street façade is so deep that it looks like a core sampling, almost an optical illusion.

The Barclay-Vesey's key departure was to present the skyscraper as an arrangement of masses. The façade is reduced to a surface of shallow, buff-brick pilasters, a continuous wrapping for the volume it contains, the aesthetic promoted by Le Corbusier. But Walker was less of a purist than his Internationalist counterparts; the Barclay-Vesey is playfully decorated with

zoomorphic figures in machine-cast stone. Babar-like elephant heads gaze out from the cornices, and ram's heads and pineapple tops decorate the crown. American wildlife combined with flora and fauna from around the world symbolize the company's role in long-distance communications. The landmarked lobby is a splendid display of Art Deco decoration. At the center of the gilded ceiling panels depicting historical scenes is an image of the acme of technology in 1927: a stand-up Bell telephone with the earpiece hanging on a hook.

Today, it is a bit difficult to comprehend the impact of the Barclay-Vesey, which looks pebble-sized at the foot of the World Trade Center. The year after it was completed, it was given the Architectural League of New York's prestigious Gold Medal, the first modern design in the city to win the award. Raymond Hood celebrated: "The modernist has always been the underdog, but when a distinctly modern structure like the new telephone building wins the League's gold medal of honor, his position and that of the classicist has been reversed."

[1] Elephant heads, pineapples, and sunflowers adorn the Barclay-Vesey's crown.

Fred F. French Building

551 FIFTH AVENUE » FRED F. FRENCH CO., H. DOUGLAS IVES, AND SLOAN & ROBERTSON, 1927

NOW THAT the modernists held sway over New York's skyline, architects sought to overthrow the axioms of Beaux-Arts design. Jazz Age architects experimented with brilliant polychromy in reaction to what they saw as the sterile whiteness of classical revival. (Of course, Greek temples in their time were riotously colorful; it was only the leaching effects of time that made them seem so pale.)

The architects for the headquarters of the Fred F. French real-estate company looked back to mist-enshrouded Babylon for inspiration, not only for its dazzling glazed polychromy and bold decorative motifs, but for the jagged ziggurat profiles of its architecture. The developer Fred French, who had a penchant for the occult, commissioned brilliantly colored terra-cotta murals for the crown of his 38-story office headquarters, the tallest building on Fifth Avenue

when it was completed. In low-relief faïence, griffins face each other across a vermilion rising sun, flanked by golden beehives against a spring-green background. The symbolism was overt, as deciphered by H. Douglas Ives, the in-house architect for the French Company: "The central motif of the large panels on the north and south sides is a rising sun, progress, flanked on either side by two winged griffins, integrity and watchfulness. At either end are two beehives with golden bees, the symbols of thrift and industry. The panels on the east and west sides contain heads of Mercury, the messenger, spreading the message of the French Plan." (The image of Mercury, the god of commerce, was applied with almost superstitious abandon throughout midtown.)

A 17-story-tall slab, only two bays wide, rises straight from a multitude of small setbacks grouped at its foot to a triplex penthouse, an unusual and visually distinctive interpretation of the setback envelope. Set on a lot only 79 by 200 feet, the French Building was codesigned by Ives and Sloan & Robertson, who also built the Chanin Building, another thin slab set on a base. The russet-brick façade is richly trimmed in limestone and polychromatic faïence at the cornices. The French Building is also one of the first Deco skyscrapers with a flat roof, anticipating the look of Internationalist slabs. (The capping sunburst mosaic may also be the world's most elaborate disguise for a water tower.)

With its bronze lobby motifs patterned after the Gate of Ishtar, the French Building was the most literal interpretation yet of Manhattan as a Babylon on the Hudson. Kneeling oxen decorate the capitals of the revolving door. The bas-relief bronze panels of the elevator doors depict a bricklayer against a background of pyramid-topped, setback towers and a bare-breasted woman holding aloft an architect's model of a setback building. Fred French did not consider it grandiose to compare himself to the fabled builder Nebuchadnezzar II by building a

Babylonian tower in his own name. As the inscription of the original Ishtar Gate reads: "I hung doors of cedar adorned with bronze at all the gate openings. I placed wild bulls and ferocious dragons in the gateways and thus adorned them with luxurious splendor so that people might gaze on them in wonder."

[1] The slab's lateral orientation influenced later adjacent towers on Fifth Avenue.   [2] The tower seems to incorporate a miniature skyline at its base.

Beekman Tower

(originally Panhellenic Tower)

3 MITCHELL PLACE » JOHN MEAD HOWELLS, 1928

J OHN MEAD HOWELL'S power-
fully vertical Beekman Tower is the lineal
descendant of Hood & Howell's Chicago
Tribune Building and Hood's American
Radiator Building, fused with Eliel Saarinen's
"astylar" entry for the Tribune competition. The
23-story tower jumps straight from its three-story
base in a series of unbroken piers.

Prominently situated on a corner site
against an open sky, the setbacks seem to taper
into lofty distances. The impact of the silhouette
is striking for the building's relatively low height.
Square windows with plain spandrels are set
behind deep reveals that look as if they have
been gouged into a clay surface with a palette
knife. From oblique angles, the windows disappear entirely, so that the whole structure seems
to be composed of blind masonry piers. The
Beekman is a fulfillment of Harvey Wiley
Corbett's prediction that under the new zoning
code the architect would become a "sculptor in
building masses," and of the artist Hugh Ferriss's
vision that buildings were meant to be "crude
clay for architects."

As with Hood's American Radiator
Building, the shaft's chamfered corners make the
eye read the orange-brick façade as a continuous
surface. At the same time, monolithic framing
piers at the corners—windowless except for a
single bay on the beveled angle—add to an
appearance of stone-like solidity. The tower is
set in from the corner by a curious three-story,
four-bay ell that connects it to an inconspicu-
ous, similarly styled 10-story wing so that the
main tower appears to be freestanding.

Originally called the Panhellenic Tower,
the building was designed as an apartment
hotel and clubhouse for female college graduates
who were members of Greek letter societies.
Symbolic Greek letters are embedded in the
base. It now functions as a suite hotel, with
12.5-foot-deep tower rooms encircling the central elevator core. Ornamentation is reduced to
round-headed windows in the base, surmounted
by frozen-fountain motifs in cast stone. The
crown features an open arcade that resembles
bubbles in the corona of a fountain, but the cornices of the setbacks are starkly undecorated,
except for a slight battering, a development that
would in turn influence Hood's Daily News
Building. The surface of orange brick is wonderfully responsive to the qualities of New York
light—sharply etched in the morning and
warmly lambent at sunset. Recessed spotlights in
the crown add a touch of Gothic mystery at
night. A more recent addition of a glassed-in
restaurant, the Top of the Tower, complicates the
last setback at the twenty-sixth floor, but the
original outlines can still be determined.

[1] A low annex, left, sets off the Beekman Tower from neighboring buildings.

Tudor City

EAST 40TH TO EAST 43RD STREETS, BETWEEN FIRST AND SECOND AVENUES » H. DOUGLAS IVES, 1928

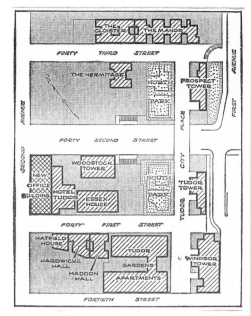

DEVELOPED BY the Fred F. French real-estate company, Tudor City was the first residential skyscraper enclave in the world. Ensconced on a naturally occurring bluff overlooking what was then New York's slaughterhouse district, the five-acre site comprises seven apartment buildings, with four 10-story apartments flanking a phalanx of three central 22-story towers on the east side. The Woodstock Tower, an apartment hotel on East 42nd Street, is the tallest at 32 stories. Overall, the complex was built to house 2,200 families, but the scale is right; the buildings are neither overwhelmingly tall, nor are there too many of them.

French succeeded in luring middle-class residents to the gritty east midtown area by dressing up his high rises in the familiar garb of Tudor styling, which bespoke history, tradition, and comfort. Tudor was an apt symbol for the middle class because the era represented a shift from medieval living to the pleasures of domesticity. The style had a strong hold on the public imagination in the 1920s, with private enclaves such as Pomander Walk (which was actually patterned after the stage sets of a play of the same name) being built on the Upper West Side. Tudor styling was also popular in newly emerging suburbs, and carried associations of trees, lawns, and privacy. The apartments were rented on the concept that midtown office workers could now walk to work rather than commute.

The styling of red brick trimmed with terra-cotta ornament on four-story limestone bases softens the blunt outlines of the towers and brings them down to a human scale. The mullioned windows are small-paned, with stained-glass insets, lending a fantasy air to the whole. From the distance, roofline sculptures of unicorns and lions holding stiff pennants enliven the silhouette.

Whatever the limitations of historicism, Tudor City functions wonderfully as a neighborhood—at day's end, kids Rollerblade on the nearly private, dead-end street of Tudor City Place, and the pleasantly landscaped, handkerchief-sized park is used by bench-sitters and dog walkers at all hours. There are many proprietary "eyes upon the street," in Jane Jacobs's phrase, from shopkeepers to restaurant diners and the flow of residents, one of the key elements that make a neighborhood safe. The complex has a small-town feel, with its own tiny post office and ZIP code, and a half-timbered, Tudor-style church, the Church of the Covenant, at the foot of the Woodstock Tower.

Tudor City literally turns its back on the environs of the East River. The walls facing the river on First Avenue are blank brick with windows only for stairwells because the original view of Manhattan's abattoirs was unsightly and, in summer, malodorous. In the late nineteenth century, the neighborhood was notorious for its criminal gangs, and was nicknamed Corcoran's Roost. The gang leader, Paddy Corcoran, is memorialized in a Gothic inscription above the entrance of the central Tudor Tower.

[1] Tudor City's landscaping creates an intimate urban enclave.   [2] Historicist detailing gives a domestic feel to the three central towers.   [3] Many faces of the '20s: the Daily News and Chrysler Buildings seen from Tudor City.

Hearst Magazine Building

(originally International Magazine Building)

959 EIGHTH AVENUE » JOSEPH URBAN, 1928

ADDITION, NORMAN FOSTER, 2005

NORMAN FOSTER'S work with Buckminster Fuller is evident in the geodesic-shaped panels of his steel-and-glass, chrysalis-like 2004 addition to the base of Joseph Urban's platform, left unfinished in 1928 because of some bad real-estate investments by William Randolph Hearst. The height of the 42-story, 496-foot tower is disguised by massive girders that exaggerate the x-bracing of a tall building and provide exciting contours. A clerestory between the Art Deco plinth and the tower makes a bold postmodern composition.

Joseph Urban's platform gave New Yorkers one of their first looks at what would later be termed the Art Deco style. Deco is actually a rubric that jumbles together many styles, from the streamlined modern classicism of the 1925 Exposition des Arts Décoratifs et Industriels Modernes in Paris to the moody lighting and disorienting angles of German Expressionism and the more abstract experiments of the Wiener Werkstätte and of the work of Charles Rennie Mackintosh.

Best known in New York for his uncompromisingly modern design for the New School for Social Research (1931), Urban was the foremost representative of the Viennese design school of the Wiener Werkstätte. When his arts and crafts shop in New York failed, Urban worked as a set designer for Hearst's extravagant silent film epics such as *When Knighthood Was in Flower* (1922), which cost an unheard-of $1.5 million and made a star of Hearst's paramour, Marion Davies.

The Hearst Magazine Building was meant to be the flagship of a vast entertainment complex near Columbus Circle. The six-story limestone base with four massive engaged columns runs along the block-length Eighth Avenue façade between West 56th and West 57th streets, and is a charmingly literal interpretation of the aspirations of the Hearst empire in theater and communications.

Paired allegorical figures in limestone by the German sculptor Henry Kreis flank the column bases, dramatically interrupting the balustrade at the second-story cornice. A bare-torsoed athlete holding a discus and a hard-hatted workman resting on his sledgehammer represent Sport and Industry; a jester in a fool's cap and a gloom-ridden tragedian depict Comedy and Tragedy; a musician with a lyre and a statue in classical armor stand for Music and Art; and a bearded man with an iron hand-press and a cowled woman with two owls stand for Printing and the Sciences. The adorable owls could have flown straight off the Secession Exhibition Building in Vienna (1898) by Joseph Maria Olbrich, who was one of Urban's teachers in Vienna.

The sculptures are a fascinating example of how neatly modern classical motifs overlaid classical designs: the figures' robes are cut in lightning-like zigzags, and the deeply fluted columns terminate in streamlined Greek urns. Here was a style that was unified and contemporary and did not directly evoke the past. The most direct influence of the Hearst Building can be seen in the base of the Empire State Building, which also features a heroic colonnade of limestone pilasters and three-quarter-round columns flanking the main entrance. In both buildings, the pillars do not suggest support, but rather epic scale, and add volume and the visual interest of light and shadow to the base.

Joseph Urban and the European modern classicists brought a boldly theatrical sensibility to American architecture. The streamlined statues on the Hearst Building even resemble their distant stylistic cousin, the Oscar statuette.

[1] Metamorphosis in metal: Norman Foster's steel-and-glass tower takes shape above Joseph Urban's 1928 base.

Chanin Building

122 EAST 42ND STREET » SLOAN & ROBERTSON, 1928

Irwin S. Chanin, a prominent developer who was also involved in the theater, explicitly stated the theme of his eponymous office building to be the "mise en scène for the romantic drama of American business." Built as leaseable office space, the Chanin Building had many theatrical touches: a private, double-height 200-seat theater in silver and black on the fiftieth floor; and a jazzy, orange-and-white-tiled Egyptian bath with brass fixtures and etched glass shower panels, which Chanin delighted in showing to visitors. In the lobby, bronze frames surrounding the shop entrances part like proscenium curtains. An underground bus terminal featured an electrically operated revolving platform.

The Chanin presents itself as the pinnacle of creation. A bronze frieze at street level depicts the evolution of life from sea to land and ultimately to the air in the form of flying birds. Flight, and by association the skyscraper, was now the ultimate symbol of modernism. Bas-reliefs of flying birds on the elevator panels welcome passengers to their skyward journey. An 18-foot-high, terra-cotta frieze of giant-scaled Deco foliate patterns that wraps around the fourth floor of the façade proclaims that this is a building of the twentieth century. The gorgeously wrought French Deco lobby, designed by Jacques Delamarre and with bronze reliefs and grilles by the architectural sculptor René Chambellan, depicts New York as the "City of Opportunity" and tells the story of the rise of Irwin Chanin. According to one contemporary critic, the theme was to show the "mental and physical processes by which an individual in New York City may rise from a humble beginning to wealth and influence by the power of his own mind and hands," with allegorical figures representing Enlightenment, Vision, Courage, and Achievement along with Endurance, Activity, Effort, and Success.

THE CHANIN'S astylar silhouette was influenced by Eliel Saarinen, but its decorative motifs are straight out of Ayn Rand. The 56-story tower's blunt-buttressed crown became a symbol of New York's crushing modernist drive, as seen in photomontages by the Russian artists Eliezer Lissitzky and Aleksandr Rodchenko. The buff-brick, limestone, and terra-cotta tower is a fascinating synthesis of skyscraper styles. The giant limestone buttresses at the base and crown are a concise reference to the skyscraper's stylistic origins in the Gothic cathedral. At the same time, the 680-foot-tall shaft that rises uninterrupted for 22 stories above a series of shallow setbacks is essentially the Internationalist slab form that would predominate after the war. The thinness of the slab on the corner site as viewed from uptown or downtown creates a classic Art Deco setback silhouette, a two-in-one solution that is echoed in Raymond Hood's McGraw-Hill Building and Rockefeller Center. The crown, reverse-lit at night so that the buttresses are thrown into shadow and the recesses are illuminated, is a realization of the Expressionist fantasies of architects Bruno Taut and Paul Scheerbart.

[1] The Chanin's original fixtures are well preserved.   [2] A revolving electric turntable once moved commuter buses underneath the Chanin.   [3] Modern times: clocks were always a central feature of public spaces.

One Fifth Avenue

HARVEY WILEY CORBETT, 1929

OOMING OVER the sedate, four-story Greek Revival flats of Washington Square, One Fifth Avenue's tapering, setback silhouette represents the ascendancy of the Art Deco style in the popular imagination. Sophisticated New Yorkers no longer needed the trappings of the past to feel at home in the twentieth century.

In One Fifth Avenue, the "shadow brick" piers that Harvey Wiley Corbett used for the party walls of his Bush Tower a decade earlier become the central message of the façade. Two-dimensional trompe l'oeil piers are limned in two-tone brick, so that the darker brick seems to be a shadow cast by projecting triangular masonry. Corbett reveals his conjurer's trick in the finials that project beyond the parapets, which are plainly two-dimensional, colored stone. Streamlined limestone gargoyles reinforce the sketchy impression of the trimmings. By reducing historicist detailing to a cartoon, the design architect Corbett announced the supremacy of modernism.

Set on a corner site among low buildings, the 27-story building is distinguished by its massing and in particular its setback silhouette, rather than its vestigial styling, nominally Venetian or Byzantine. Chamfered corners add a sense of lithic solidity. At the setbacks, corbeled blind arcades demarcate the cornices. The massive Fifth Avenue front, which rises for 17 stories, is organized into eight bays above a four-story limestone base with bracketed limestone balconies. The balustrades of the balconies are tiny Doric columns, anticipating the 12 tree-like fluted Doric columns in the severe, double-tiered, oak-paneled lobby. A sleek, frameless Deco lobby clock set directly onto the paneling epitomizes Corbett's modernistic updating of historicist styles.

Corbett wanted to establish a visual landmark for the base of Fifth Avenue, so the building is remarkably contextual. The octagonal chimney around which the wings are massed

forms a campanile-like image against the open sky of Washington Square Park, and even the silhouette of a sloped roof split by a chimney can be seen as a reference to the older Federal style houses of Greenwich Village. The stripped-down Doric lobby is a neat overlay for the Greek Revival mansion that formerly occupied the site.

Real estate ads in the *New Yorker* magazine of August 1927 touted terraced apartments, 17-foot by 28-foot living rooms, and depicted the tower dwarfing Stanford White's Beaux-Arts monument of Washington Square Arch at its foot. Unfortunately, a botched restoration of the tower's brown brickwork has left a piebald result, so it is difficult to discern the architect's original visual pun of reducing historicist detail to a two-dimensional graphic image.

[1] Though modernistic in style. One Fifth also appealed to picturesque sensibilities. [2] One Fifth was a bold, early expression of the setback silhouette.

Helmsley Building

(originally New York Central Building)

EVEN THOUGH Beaux-Arts ornamentation no longer makes sense at skyscraper scale, the Helmsley Building, like its forerunner the Municipal Building, is so graciously urban that you almost don't notice. The best part of Beaux-Arts design in terms of its civic function is the clarity of its parti—you always know where you stand, and what all the parts of the building are for. The building originally served as the headquarters of the New York Central railroad companies. Warren & Wetmore unobtrusively resolved the siting's complex challenges: the 1.2 million-square-foot building reroutes vehicular traffic on Park Avenue through raised viaducts, provides through-block walkways for pedestrians, complements the style of the monumentality of Grand Central Terminal, and presents a visual capstone to Park Avenue.

The separation of vehicular and pedestrian traffic has been a feature of the ideal city dating back to Leonardo da Vinci, but the Pershing Viaduct that connects the two halves of Park Avenue is one of the few working examples in existence today. Balustrades hide the cars until they disappear into overscaled Georgian arches at the second-story level, and then debouch onto Park Avenue below a gilded, ornamental clock flanked by figures of Mercury and Ceres (representing the business of shipping grain by rail) by the sculptor Edward McCartan.

The 34-story, 567-foot-tall, buff-brick and limestone building features 15-story, U-shaped wings, and a gilded, oval-dormered, pyramidal roof that is surmounted by a copper-clad lantern. Even critics of the day considered the building's ornamental motifs hopelessly *retardataire*. In a 1930 article in *Architectural Forum*, Thomas Tallmadge snickered: "Classic columns, chased out of New York's thoroughfares, are reported to have take a final refuge on the top story of the New York Central Building." The bracketed colonnade of eight three-story-tall Corinthian limestone columns supports nothing

in turn but another pair of brackets, violating the visual sense of weight.

Nonetheless, the grand, Louis XIV-style lobby, paneled in glossy travertine and trimmed in jaspé Oriental marble, provides a palace for the people and celebrates the prestige of the railroads. The iconography of winged wheels emerging from cloud banks is as strange as anything Magritte could have conceived. Above the elevator doors, bronze reliefs depict a winged helmet surrounding a globe, symbolizing the American empire's global reach. Lightning bolts and pickaxes represent electricity and labor, the power behind the railroads. Steel wheels surrounded by sheaths of wheat burst forth in cornucopias, symbolizing the bounty of American agriculture carried by rail. The rococo gloire is a marvelously syncretic image, at once resembling a baroque sunburst and an abstract Art Deco skyline. On the exterior, the piers end in giant, terra-cotta buffalo heads, connoting the railroad's connection with the West. Alas, the gilded cage elevators with their heavenly blue domes that resembled Victorian birdcages, have been remodeled.

[1] The pyramidal roof, under construction, provides a visual capstone to Park Avenue.

Fuller Building

AFTER EXPERIMENTING with low massing, Walker & Gillette arrived at the classic Art Deco silhouette in their Fuller Building, which was until recently the headquarters of the Fuller Construction Company. Here, the skyscraper form is codified into a wide, multiuse base that conforms to the street cornice; a relatively unornamented, slender shaft for prime office space; and a signature decorative crown.

One of the first tall buildings north of midtown, the 40-story Fuller Building's striking, black-and-white Deco/Aztec crown, prominently sited on the northeast corner of Madison Avenue and East 57th Street, can be seen for great distances. Story-tall oculi framed in monochromatic sunburst patterns look out over the city in three directions, and are surmounted by a triple setback crown capped with black terra cotta in vibrant motifs of zigzags and triangles.

The six-story base, framed in black granite, contains luxury shops and galleries. Eight bays of Chicago-style windows on the 57th Street front provide light for the galleries. The thin tower slab, clad in light-colored stone with smaller fenestration, contains offices, and the boldly decorated crown accented by three-sided balconies is the Fuller headquarters, still one of the largest construction companies in the country.

By the late 1920s, modern classicism (or Deco, as we now call it) was well accepted by the public as the contemporary style, and no longer had to state its case so emphatically. Historicist ornament is transformed into two-dimensional representation. In place of a typical classical columned entrance, the Fuller Building features flat pilasters with two-dimensional black-granite triangles instead of capitals, and lines to represent fluting. The cornices of the upper setbacks suggest crenellations in patterns of black-and-white terra cotta.

The sculptural clock above the entry by Elie Nadelman in black Swedish granite and white Rockwood stone is a syncretic image of classical and modern classical motifs: two classically garbed workmen rest on their sledgehammers, flanking an octagonal clock against an abstract skyline of setback towers.

The lobby celebrates the achievements of the Fuller Company in its floor mosaics: the Tacoma Building in 1889, the first all-steel structure; the Fuller Flatiron Building, here given its rarely used full name; and the Fuller Building itself, in a schematic black-and-white representation with shaded blue tile. Bronze elevator door panels form a tableau of the building trades: a workman "rides the ball" of a swinging derrick; bricklayers set bricks with mortarboards; plasterers lay up laths; stone masons set blocks with a tackle; pneumatic drill operators chip out the foundation; carpenters frame out the rooms; and pipe fitters adjust the plumbing.

[1] Setback skyscrapers were also appreciated for their picturesque qualities.   [2] The Fuller's classically styled workers rest before an abstract Art Deco skyline.

Williamsburgh Savings Bank Tower

(now Republic National Bank)

1 HANSON PLACE, BROOKLYN »

HALSEY, MCCORMACK & HELMER, 1929

Brooklyn's Beacon of Service

The largest four-dial timepiece in the world

AT the Gateway to Long Island, *Telechron* because of its accuracy and dependability, was selected from among all other types of clocks to broadcast Observatory Time from the tower of the new home of the Williamsburgh Savings Bank.

To the millions of commuters who yearly use the Long Island Railroad to carry them to and from their Long Island homes and to the residents of Brooklyn, this huge *Telechron* tower clock will render a time service second to none.

ELECTIME CORPORATION · 396 LIVINGSTON ST. BROOKLYN, N.Y. · *Telechron* · WARREN TELECHRON CO. ASHLAND, MASS.

B Y T H E end of the 1920s, the setback skyscraper, originally built in response to a New York zoning code, became a style that caught on from Chicago to Shanghai. The slender spire of the former Williamsburgh Savings Bank is one of the best examples of the style, and was meant to put Brooklyn on the map as a rival to Manhattan in terms of both architecture and finance.

The iconography of pre–World War II skyscrapers is charmingly literal: the 30-story, 512-foot-tall Williamsburgh Savings Bank Tower is a Byzantine basilica devoted to the virtues of thrift. Its six-story limestone base above rainbow granite at street level abounds with savings motifs: cagey lions guard a padlocked strongbox with the bank's initials, squirrels store up nuts, and bees zoom over a beehive surmounted by a head of Mercury.

The procession through the grand, 128-foot-long, 72-foot-wide, and 63-foot-high vaulted banking room is an allegorical journey. At the gates, modern classical metal figures by Réné Chambellan depict the trades of the bank's immigrant savers: a fruit seller, a mechanic, a cook, and a carpenter (a capital inside the bank depicts a sewing-machine operator). The cast-stone capitals of the columns demonstrate reasons to save: a woman with her hair in a bun and a strongbox symbolizes security in old age, while a man with a long beard reading a scroll shows a happy retirement. The real incentive is the immigrants' dream, that their children can enter the professional classes: a woman reading by the lamp of knowledge stands for education; and two young men, one contemplating a model train and the other with a caduceus, represent engineers and doctors. The gold-mosaic, barrel-vault ceiling adorned with symbols of the zodiac glitters like a dream of future riches. Banks wanted to impress the public with their wealth and security, so the chamber is paved in marmoreal splendor: 22 kinds of marble, from dark purple to green and

veined red were used in the richly patterned Cosmatesque floor.

The slender tower projecting from a slab-like platform dominates downtown Brooklyn like a medieval castle. It was the tallest structure on Long Island for 60 years, until the 48-story, 663-foot Citicorp office building was completed in Hunters Point, Queens, in 1989. The Williamsburgh's four-sided clock tower, with clock faces measuring 27 feet in diameter, was the world's largest when it was built. The gilded copper dome was the bank's symbol, modeled after the original bank designed by George B. Post at 175 Broadway in 1875 (also a New York City landmark), which was the inspiration for the tower's Byzantine and Romanesque styling.

The tower's sense of height is accentuated by the narrow 2:1 proportions of the platform, which consists of 10 bays of two windows each on the Ashland Place front and five bays on Hanson Place. The centrally massed, buff-brick and terra-cotta tower rises almost sheerly from the Ashland front except for a few shallow setbacks, but sets back dramatically from the sides of the platform. The Williamsburgh has the surrounding sky all to itself. Unfortunately, the arcaded twenty-sixth-floor observatory—with unimpeded views in four directions of the Manhattan skyline and Brooklyn's low blocks, punctuated by church steeples—is now closed to the public.

[1] The tower was meant to anchor a new urban hub that never quite took off.   [2] The grand banking floor was designed to inspire Brooklyn's immigrants with respect for savings.

Downtown Athletic Club

19 WEST STREET » STARRETT & VAN VLECK, 1930

THE EXTREMELY tall and narrow, 35-story, 534-foot-tall Downtown Athletic Club is the apotheosis of the Art Deco skyscraper aesthetic, because each floor is devoted to a different function. A regulation boxing ring takes up most of the eighteenth floor; there is a full-court basketball gym on eight; a four-lane, Olympic-sized pool on 12, and a rooftop sun deck with panoramic views in three directions. In its heyday, the club even featured a landscaped indoor miniature golf course. As Rem Koolhaas writes in his indispensable *Delirious New York*, "nature is now resurrected *inside* the Skyscraper as merely one of its infinite layers."

The club is a dizzying fantasia that lifts all the aspects of urban living into the clouds, just as the earliest skyscraper theorists had imagined. The top 15 floors are devoted to 111 hotel rooms for sky-dwellers—tiny, ocean-liner-like cabins with spectacular views of the harbor. Every form of recreation is provided for—billiards, banquets, massage, squash courts—each on a different level connected by banks of elevators. The swimming pool, under a double-height ceiling, is the pièce de résistance. Koolhaas captures the over-the-top aim of the architects: "At night, the pool is illuminated only by its underwater lighting system, so that the entire slab of water, with its frenetic swimmers, appears to float in space, suspended between the electric scintillation of the Wall Street towers and the stars reflected in the Hudson."

The enigmatic exterior of variegated orange-glazed brick gives little hint of the exclusive (if somewhat dated) luxuries within (the club was all-male until 1972). There are no windows at street level on the narrow, 78-foot, 8-inch-wide West Street front, and the frontispiece above the entry consists only of unetched limestone blocks. The platform is fortress-like; in fact the window bays do not even begin until the eighth floor. This is a building whose architectural plan is only for the initiated.

The tower springs up in three major setbacks, minimally highlighted with limestone copings, and ends in a Gothic-style turret that conceals a water tank. The only decorative touches are metal-trimmed chevrons in the windows and glass spandrels, painted an opaque rust brown. The window bays are continuous glazed strips suppressed behind uninterrupted brick piers. Though not quite as plush as it was in the 1930s, when six barbers waited on call and a raw oyster bar adjoined the locker room, the club is still devoted to the manly pleasures of Clubman talc, Shine-O-Mat automatic shoeshine machines, and proper decorum: "congregating in the Lobby area with athletic attire is strictly forbidden." A charming detail: the club's emblem of a diving seagull over the harbor shows a skyline of close-packed, flat-roofed towers rather than fanciful geometric shapes—a vision of the city as it actually became.

[1] A stylish woman of the 1930s passes the club's cryptic exterior.   [2] The starkly undecorated tower rises over its historically detailed neighbors.

Daily News Building

220 EAST 42ND STREET AT SECOND AVENUE » RAYMOND HOOD AND JOHN MEAD HOWELLS, 1930

THE 36-STORY, 476-foot, two-inch-tall Daily News Building was one of the first skyscrapers in the world with a virtually unornamented top and cornices, a prototype for the postwar Internationalist office building. The white-brick piers of the Daily News simply come to a halt at the setbacks without decoration, as if they had been clipped off. Hood insisted this was a result of pragmatism: "I tried the simple expedient of stopping without searching for or causing the owner to pay for an effect." The depth of the slab was a response to the desirable 27-foot

throw of light from the windows, and the fenestration was determined by the width of a window that a typical office worker could open with ease (Hood calculated 4.5 feet) in an era before air-conditioning.

Despite the boldly modernist gesture of undecorated vertical strips, Hood was unable to give up a vestigial Gothic leaning that he inherited from his training with the great American Gothic revivalists Ralph Adams Cram and Bertram Goodhue. The red-and-black-brick spandrels taper slightly back at the cornices, so that the piers seem to stand out, like the crenellations of a Gothic tower.

Hood arrived at the asymmetrical massing by carving away at plasticene blocks, rather than using the more common renderings. But unlike Ralph Walker and Hugh Ferriss, Hood did not romanticize the skyscraper as a carved mountain. The skin of the Daily News Building is paper-thin, plainly a façade of bricks hung on a steel skeleton. Its lack of mass emphasizes the abstract arrangement of its components. Hood also abandoned the model of a tall building as a classical column in favor of a grouping of slab-like forms.

Critics at the time still found a bit of *architecture parlant* in the design, and remarked that the white piers looked like bundled newspapers hot off the press. An even more literal interpretation of the building's color scheme might be the punch line of the old joke, "What's black and white and read all over?" Hood specified red window shades in the multiple, repeating bays.

The three-story, pierced-granite tableau over the entrance depicts a 1920s street scene under a city of towering skyscrapers. The period details are wonderful—tycoons stroll by in top hats, women in cloches, and a boy in knickers. The Daily News Building itself is presented as a *stadtkröne*, or crown of the city, with the sun rising behind the tower. This image is a direct descendant of the Gothic cathedral as the symbol and image of the city, and a link with the heavens.

The lobby, with its faceted dome lined in black glass above a sunken globe, is an Expressionist dream straight out of Superman comics. The "ten-foot terrestrial globe," eerily lit from below, spins in the black chamber, meant to suggest the void of space. Brass dials keep track of the temperature and wind speed, while points in the spiraling, sloping terrazzo floor mark off distances and directions of major cities (Beijing is 6,882 miles due west). A 1960 annex by Harrison & Abramovitz blends in tastefully, matching the wide plate-glass look of the original entrance.

[1] The cornices are unornamented, a radical step at the time.   [2] The Expressionist black grotto of the Daily News lobby evokes infinite space.   [3] Hugh Ferriss's rendering would be a suitable home for Superman's DAILY PLANET.

40 Wall Street

(originally the Bank of Manhattan Company Building)

H. CRAIG SEVERANCE

AND YASUO MATSUI, 1930

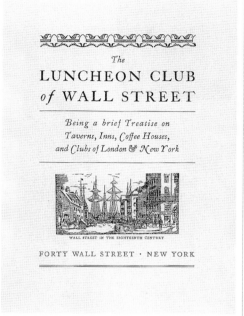

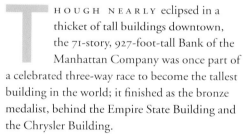

The
LUNCHEON CLUB
of WALL STREET

*Being a brief Treatise on
Taverns, Inns, Coffee Houses,
and Clubs of London & New York*

WALL STREET IN THE EIGHTEENTH CENTURY

FORTY WALL STREET · NEW YORK

THOUGH NEARLY eclipsed in a thicket of tall buildings downtown, the 71-story, 927-foot-tall Bank of the Manhattan Company was once part of a celebrated three-way race to become the tallest building in the world; it finished as the bronze medalist, behind the Empire State Building and the Chrysler Building.

Forty Wall is proof of the power of symbolic ornament in making a building memorable to the public. Its setbacks and clean-lined shaft are thoroughly modern, and, from street level, the building looks just like Hugh Ferriss's bold renderings. However, the roof is *retardataire*: a French Renaissance-style, dormered pyramid topped by a lantern that gives 40 Wall the appearance of being a much older building. The pyramid was the bank's symbol, but in the 1920s, newness was everything, and 40 Wall was promptly forgotten. More recently, postmodern architects like Philip Johnson have come about 180 degrees to appreciate the picturesque qualities of such spires.

Forty Wall Street was completed in 11 months, a record-breaking feat for a building containing nearly one million square feet of floor space. The foundations were begun before the site was even cleared in May 1928 by Starrett Brothers and Eken, which also constructed the Empire State Building. New leases in New York were traditionally signed on the first of May, and the bank moved in on schedule in 1929. Overall, the building is the very model of American efficiency, from the way seven adjoining lots were secretly assembled to make up the site, to the meticulous construction schedule, the details of which include dates for applying finish carpentry and installing mail chutes.

Despite its height, 40 Wall loses much of its impact because it is a midblock site, surrealistically situated next to the mighty Greek Revival Federal Hall National Memorial. The Trump Organization acquired the building as a speculative venture in 1995, and the block-through lobby was renovated by Der Scutt with lots of marble and glittery bronze surfaces—even the simple limestone rosettes on the façade have been gilded.

[1] Wall Street's towers were refuges for a privileged few.   [2] A mason applies finishing touches to parapets below the copper crown.

Chrysler Building

405 LEXINGTON AVENUE » WILLIAM VAN ALEN, 1930

THE CHRYSLER BUILDING was built at the fever pitch of the skyscraper's delirious development before the Great Depression, when midtown Manhattan resounded with jackhammers and pile drivers. It shows the extraordinary influence of German Expressionism on skyscraper design and the frenzied push for height that consumed architects of the 1920s. In this discontinuous, postmodern age, one can only gaze in wide wonder at the Chrysler's unified symbolism as a chrysalis between automobile and flying machine.

One of New York's most entertaining buildings, the silver-hooded Chrysler Building had its origins in the amusement parks of Coney Island. A real-estate developer named William H. Reynolds, who conceived of Coney Island's Dreamland, commissioned the architect William Van Alen to design what would have otherwise been known as the Reynolds Building. Reynolds's chief contribution was insisting that the building have a metallic crown, overriding Van Alen's objections.

The 77-story Chrysler was part of a madcap, three-way dash to become the tallest building in the world. Its rivals were the now largely neglected Bank of the Manhattan Company at 40 Wall Street, designed by Van Alen's ex-partner and archrival H. Craig Severance, and the Empire State Building. When Severance got wind that the Chrysler was going to top out at 925 feet, he added a 50-foot flagpole that made his building two feet taller, at 927 feet. Then, in August 1930, Van Alen unveiled his secret weapon—the "vertex"—a spire made of chrome nickel steel that was secretly assembled inside the Chrysler's dome and raised from within to bring the building's height to 1,048 feet. Van Alen's vertex had the distinction of being the first man-made structure to top the 1,024.5-foot-tall Eiffel Tower, which had reigned in solitary grandeur since the Paris World's Fair of 1889.

The Empire State and the Chrysler each had their own in-house photographer to publicize the race to the top. Lewis Hine took dramatic, social-realist-style pictures of the workmen poised vertiginously in the clouds for the Empire State. Margaret Bourke-White captured the strange, Gothic feel of the Chrysler's silver eagle heads glaring over the city.

The Chrysler's reign as the world's tallest lasted only 11 months, until it was topped by the Empire State Building, which opened in May 1931. Without its mast, the Empire State was only two feet higher than the Chrysler, at 1,050 (a 200-foot-tall mast brought the height to 1,250 feet, and a 204-foot-tall television antenna added in 1950 brought the overall height to 1,452 feet, 8-$\frac{9}{16}$ inches, to the top of the lightning rod).

The world's record was broken again by the 110-story, 1,350-foot World Trade Towers in 1973–74, then later in 1974 by the 110-story, 1,454-foot-tall Sears Tower in Chicago. The title is currently held by Cesar Pelli's 88-story, 1,483-foot-tall Petronas Towers in Kuala Lumpur, Malaysia, soon to be topped by Shanghai's 1,509-foot World Financial Center. The Sears still has the world's highest occupiable floor, 150 feet above the Petronas's, and the world's highest elevator ride. The tallest man-made object in the world remains Toronto's 1,815-foot Canadian National Tower, completed in 1975.

The Chrysler is surely one of the strangest office buildings designed for an American corporation. Its lobby is just short of a German Expressionist stage set. Folds of black Belgian granite drape the entrances like parting proscenium curtains, and metal zigzag motifs that look as if they could have been taken from Fritz Lang's *Metropolis* run above the entrances. The triangle-shaped lobby is a dark, bizarre cavern of crystalline angles and indirect lighting behind onyx stone, more the kind of place to encounter a Valkyrie than make a business appointment. A representation of the Chrysler Building itself appears in a ceiling mural.

The original observation lounge could have been a film set for *The Cabinet of Dr.*

1

[1] This early rendering of the Chrysler Building shows an alternative crown.

Caligari with its faceted ceiling, walls painted to resemble stars emerging in an evening sky, and Saturn-shaped lighting fixtures. The double-storied Cloud Club featured unobstructed four-sided views of New York, below the Chrysler's distinctive triangular windows. In the cigar room, Prohibition-era millionaires stashed their liquor in special caches below the tobacco-colored upholstery. Walter P. Chrysler slept in baronial splendor in a Tudor-style bedroom complete with a walk-in fireplace.

The building materials are luxe and exotic—red flame-patterned Moroccan marble, whose hectic layers seem to capture the spirit of the Jazz Age, and yellow Siena marble floors. The marquetry elevator doors and cabs are exquisite, a poem to recite: teakwood, Philippine mahogany; Cuban plum-pudding wood; English gray harewood; African and South American prima vera; aspen, curly maple, and walnut from America; and Australian silky oak. The rich wood inlay is another literal representation of the automobile, because cars of the day often had wooden dashboards and trim.

Many attempts have been made to decode the Chrysler's façade, particularly the spire, which was derided by leading critics of the time as a "stunt design," with "all this inane romanticism, this meaningless voluptuousness, this void symbolism," an "upended swordfish," and as "Little Nemo architecture" referring to the futuristic comic strip. The thirty-first floor of the white-brick tower with gray-brick trim is decorated with a frieze of stylized motor cars surmounted by winged urns that evoke the radiator cap of a 1929 Chrysler automobile. At the next setback, eight giant metal eagle-head gargoyles guard the points of the compass like protective emblems on a medieval castle.

The leitmotif is of a car metamorphosing into a flying machine, or machinery becoming organic flight. Urns sprout wings, eagle heads are made of metal. In this context, the spire can be seen as a feather made of metal, with the triangular windows and patterned metal panels

2

3

4

representing barbules and rachis. Whatever it represents, Andy Warhol summed up the skyscraper's essence in an insight both profound and superficial: "They look like money."

[1] The entry's zigzag lines resemble a German Expressionist dynamoelectric generator.   [2] Car showroom on the ground floor of the Chrysler Building. 1936.   [3] Andy Warhol said of New York's silver-trimmed skyscrapers. "They look like money."   [4] 1937 model of Chrysler's Airflow sedan on display in the showroom.

San Remo Apartments

(originally San Remo Hotel)

145 AND 146 CENTRAL PARK WEST » EMERY ROTH, 1930

I N T H E San Remo Apartments, Emery Roth successfully combined nostalgia for Old World elegance with the modernist aesthetic of skyscraper living. The San Remo's Italian Renaissance styling, though pared down to a picturesque minimum, is sufficient to convey the status of its residents. Garlanded cartouches and curved broken pediments top twin entries that lead to separate towers. Inside, the small lobbies are paneled in exotic shades of beige, oxblood, and salmon marble.

Above a three-story rusticated limestone base, the massive, relatively plain platform with a 200-foot frontage on Central Park West rises to a 17-story setback. The two nearly identical 10-story towers, modeled after the Choregic Monument of Lysicrates, are what make the San Remo such a landmark on the skyline of Central Park West. There is something grandly American about doubling the image of an ancient monument: it is as if to say things are twice as good in America, which Roth, who immigrated as a penniless Hungarian orphan, no doubt believed. Magically, the towers, originally built to conceal water tanks, are doubled again in shimmering reflections in the Lake of Central Park. Like the park itself, the San Remo epitomizes the romantic nineteenth-century ideal of subordinating nature to culture. Glimpsed through stands of broad-leafed northern catalpa trees in the park, the San Remo looks like a vision of the White City idealized by the World's Columbian Exposition of 1893 in Chicago, where Roth apprenticed.

From a compositional point of view, the towers play powerfully against the background element of the sky, etching the setback image in negative space, much as Cesar Pelli's Petronas Towers do in Kuala Lumpur. Sixteen-foot-tall limestone Corinthian columns stand out against the beige-brick towers, surrounded by eight-foot-tall urns meant to be seen from the street. The finials of the illuminated copper beacons are 400 feet above the sidewalk. The palette is

1

subtly picturesque, as if daubed in watercolor: a few courses of red roof tile, beige brick, whitish limestone, tan terra cotta, and green metal railings under the green copper lanterns.

When the San Remo opened in 1930, it was advertised as the "Aristocrat of Central Park West"; however, a year later it was still one-third vacant because of the stock market crash. The duplex tower apartments shared no party walls with other apartments and offered terraced views in nearly all directions. Some living rooms are 22 by 36 feet, under 11-foot ceilings. Semiprivate elevators carried tenants to within a few feet of each apartment. Roth's biographer Steven Ruttenbaum rightly calls these residences "mansions in the clouds." The San Remo is the last of the great premodern luxury residences. Even Roth's El Dorado, completed the next year, sported finials that resemble miniature setback skyscrapers.

[1] The San Remo's romantic towers were inspired by the drum of the Choregic Monument of Lysicrates.

Riverside Church

490 RIVERSIDE DRIVE » ALLEN & COLLENS, 1930

RIVERSIDE CHURCH is New York's last great eclectic skyscraper. Even though it was completed well into the modernist era, it hearkens back to an earlier period when architects attempted to disguise their tall buildings under layers of historicist detail. Though modeled after the thirteenth-century French Gothic cathedral of Chartres and sheathed in ornately carved Indiana limestone, Riverside Church is in fact a 30-story office building. In its massing of a 10-story nave and a 392-foot-tall tower, Riverside more resembles the platform and tower of the Woolworth Building than it does Chartres. Here, Gothic historicism thus comes full circle, with a church modeled after an office building that was modeled after secular Gothic design. Because of its steel-frame construction combined with faithful copies of limestone sculpture, Riverside is the ultimate syncretic image of the skyscraper as *stadtkröne*, or medieval crown of the city.

The site is enormous, taking up two full blocks between West 120th and West 122nd Streets, bordered by Riverside Drive and Claremont Avenue. Much like the Downtown Athletic Club, Riverside exemplifies the modernist's desire to include the world under one roof, like a luxury liner, with each level providing a new experience. A cross section reveals lounges, offices, and studios in the belfry tower. Below ground is a full-length basketball court, a theater, and a four-lane bowling alley. Even the modernist yearning for unlimited transportation is catered to: there is an underground parking lot, and the tower is equipped with blinking lights for the safety of airplanes.

At the same time, Riverside is a throwback to the eclectic era in its desire to achieve monumentality. It features the world's largest carillon, weighing more than 100 tons, supported by unusually stout I beams. The carillon features the largest tuned bell ever cast. Other records are anachronistic: the 355-high observation deck is served by the tallest elevators of any church in the world. But precisely because of its scale, Riverside is lacking in monumentality. The shrimpy buttresses, which are ornamental rather than structural, are impossibly meager to support the weight of a 30-story building, so the mind scales down the height to more believable proportions. From any distance, the church commands Riverside Drive, but the closer you get to it, the more it seems to shrink.

Inside, the architects Henry C. Pelton (Columbia University, class of 1890), Charles Collens, and the chief designer Burnham Hoyt also fiddled with proportions to meet the needs of a modern church. The 215-foot-long, 89-foot-wide, 100-foot-tall nave, which seats 2,500 people, is lower and much broader than the original at Chartres, because Riverside, an interdenominational Christian church, is more oriented to the spoken sermon than the sacramental rituals of the Catholic Church. The apse is suppressed, bringing the choir and pulpit closer to the congregation, and there is no transept. Most radically, the narthex with its bank of four elevators completely resembles a modern office building rather than a church entrance. To some degree, the designers must have recognized the absurdity of cloaking a steel-cage building in Gothic drag, and used the humorous tradition of Gothic caricature to spoof the anachronisms. In a phone booth on the ground floor, two gargoyles gab into hook-and-receiver telephones, while a pig, the proverbial "hog on the line," ties up the lines.

[1] The steeple was reinforced with extra steel to bear the carillon's weight.   [2] The office tower steeple dominates Riverside Drive, but seems to dwindle as you approach it.

120 Wall Street

ELY JACQUES KAHN, 1930

KNOWN FOR his modern classicist designs, Ely Jacques Kahn's chief concern was finding a decorative style that had no reference to the past. The 1925 Exposition des Arts Décoratifs, which introduced what is now called the Art Deco style, was a turning point in his life: "There I felt that the pompous sterility of 1900 with its white lines of columns was over." At first, Kahn thought the revolution lay in brightly colored terra cotta, as in his paganly polychromatic Two Park Avenue Building (1928), but the façades of his later buildings rely more on texture and monochrome abstract patterns.

Kahn's 33-story, white-brick 120 Wall Street Building is a three-sided pyramidal setback that forms the classic "wedding-cake" tiered silhouette of a New York Deco skyscraper. In fact, its appearance is the result of closely conforming to the envelope prescribed by the 1916 Zoning Code with low masses rather than a base and tall tower. The setbacks recede in shallow formations from a massive, 16-story platform that takes up the block front on South Street between Wall and Pine Streets. The narrow building is oriented toward Wall Street because of the address's prestige. Sited at the far end of Wall Street, 120 Wall was the first of the phalanx of similarly sized skyscrapers that now line the East River on South Street.

Kahn, whose eldest sister, the artist Rena Rosenthal, was involved in the Wiener Werkstätte movement, looked to textile patterns and abstract geometrical forms as the vocabulary for his non-historicist designs. The façade of 120 Wall, composed of four bays of three windows, is integrated by subtle, textile-like variations in brick patterning. The center spandrels are horizontally coursed, with alternating flush and deeply inset bands, while the corner spandrels are recessed slightly and incised with shallow vertical lines, to form a warp and woof. "Decoration is not necessarily ornament," Kahn wrote. "The interest of an object has primarily to do with its shape, proportion and color. The texture of its surface, the rhythms of the elements that break that surface either into planes or distinct areas of contrasting interest, becomes ornament."

The materials of 120 Wall Street are rich, but spare. Polished red-granite panels frame wide-paned commercial windows at street level as part of the five-story limestone base. A gold metallic grille of pagoda-like geometric forms surmounts the entry. Relief moldings are the only feature of the gorgeous rose-marble lobby. The heavily embossed labyrinthine patterns of the nickel chrome elevator doors are fine examples of Kahn's influential modern classicist aesthetic. "The modernist uses his material so as to make it beautiful in itself," Kahn wrote. "Marble, glass, fabrics, wood, do not need applied decoration to glorify their beauty or texture. The problem, simplifying itself to a matter of form, contrast or proper use of material, now demands particular study."

The ceiling mural of the entrance depicts a syncretic image of the low village of Dutch Manhattan mirrored by a skyline of abstract setback towers. Who is to say whether some spirit of place, the pointed teepees of the original Algonquin settlement, the traditional stepped-back gables of Dutch colonial architecture, or the ubiquitous wooden water towers—which themselves resemble setback turrets—influenced modernist dreams of the future?

[1] Kahn's abstract geometrical artistry is reflected in the entrance grille.

500 Fifth Avenue

SHREVE, LAMB & HARMON, 1931

THE 58-STORY, 625-foot-tall buff-brick 500 Fifth Avenue is the plain vanilla of modern classicism. Shreve, Lamb & Harmon's asymmetrically massed tower is perhaps the closest realization of Eliel Saarinen's influential "styleless" entry for the Chicago Tribune competition because it has almost no overt historicist references.

Built by the same architects who did the Empire State Building, in the same year, and on an equally prominent site on the northwest corner of 42nd Street, 500 Fifth Avenue nonetheless remains virtually anonymous. This is in part due its scale; the plot of 500 Fifth is less than a quarter the size of the Empire State, so the setbacks have less impact. But the lack of symbolic decoration cannot be discounted as the main reason for the lack of public recognition. The flat crown, which once featured the giant red numerals 500, is now just an exposed cooling tower. The tower lacks both the distinctive spire of the Empire State Building, and its dramatic contrast between plinth and shaft. In 500 Fifth, surface ornament and even the setbacks themselves become vestigial, so the emphasis is on the slab of the sheer, square-topped tower, a forerunner of the postwar office building. Shallow setbacks on the corner street fronts lead to a flush party wall on the uptown side that runs the entire length of the building.

The four-story limestone base of 500 Fifth is minimally decorated with celadon-colored metal spandrels, and incised foliate and frozen-fountain motifs in shallow relief. The cornices of the shallow setbacks are accented with tan panels of abstract-patterned terra cotta, and a central bay of dark stone spandrels runs up the center of the Fifth Avenue and 42nd Street fronts. The only nod to the skyscraper's grandiose self-image of the period is a relief of a gilded modern classical female figure above the entry, delicately fingering an architect's model of the building itself.

Inside, the lobby is almost shorn of ornament. The walls consist of pink-gray matched marble with little trim, under recessed lights. The only historicist touch is a pair of griffins that support the lobby clock. Without references to the past, the setback itself becomes the leitmotif, repeated in the base, and in the glass-and-bronze entryway. As the Exposition des Arts Décoratifs of 1925 mandated: "Reproductions, imitations and counterfeits of ancient styles will be strictly prohibited." The next step was clear: architects looked at such a building and realized that little else needed to be removed in order to reduce architecture to its fundamentals of form, massing, volume, and structure.

[1] Starrett Company workers were renowned for putting up their buildings in record time.   [2] The entrance of 500 Fifth Avenue, right, is the façade's most decorative feature.   [3] The asymmetrical tower rises over "the most congested traffic section in the world."

Empire State Building

350 FIFTH AVENUE » SHREVE, LAMB & HARMON, 1931

THE EMPIRE STATE BUILDING is the archetypal skyscraper, the one to which all others must inevitably be compared. Its silhouette of a broad, 197-by-425-foot platform; low, massed setbacks; free-standing tower; and romantic, winged spire can be recognized in a thousand tchotchkes, from pencil erasers to key-chain thermometers. It is perhaps the ultimate example of the skyscraper as *stadtkröne*, the crown of the city, which derives from the tradition of the Gothic cathedral. The lobby is dominated by a marble panel with aluminum relief that depicts the Empire State with the sun rising behind its mast.

But as the architectural historian Carol Willis makes clear in her iconoclastic book, *Form Follows Finance*, the renowned parti was determined as much by economic considerations as by architectural design. William Lamb, the chief designer, tersely summed up the plan he was given:

The program was short enough—a fixed budget, no space more than 28 feet from window to corridor, as many stories of such space as possible, an exterior of limestone, and completion date of May 1, 1931, which meant a year and six months from the beginning of the sketches.

The configuration of base, setbacks, and shaft was largely determined by the grouping of the elevators in the core, and the arrangement of floor space so that no office was more than 28 feet from a window, to maintain a desirable level of natural lighting. Again, Lamb presents the concept with admirable clarity:

The logic of the plan is very simple. A certain amount of space in the center, arranged as compactly as possible, contains the vertical circulation, toilets, shafts and corridors. Surrounding this is a perimeter of office space 28 feet deep. The sizes of the floors diminish as the elevators decrease in number. . . . The four groups of high-rise elevators are placed in the center of the building with low-rise

1

[1] A misguided army B-25 bomber struck the building on July 28, 1945, killing 14.

1

2

3

4

groups adjoining on the east and west sides so that, as these drop off, the building steps back from the long dimension of the property to approach the square form of the shaft, with the result that instead of being a tower set upon a series of diminishing set-backs prescribed by the zoning law, the building becomes all tower rising from a great five-story base.

The construction statistics are stupendous: 10 million bricks, 1,172 miles of elevator cable, 2 million feet of electrical wire, and 200,000 cubic feet of stone assembled by 3,500 workers in 18 months, with five deaths. The building rose at an average of four and a half floors a week; in one crescendo of construction, 14 and a half floors were built in 10 days. Lunch stands serving hot food, sandwiches, "near beer," and ice cream were installed at five different levels to save workers the considerable time of descending to the streets. R. H. Shreve concluded: "The simplicity of the structure and its freedom from numerous small and relatively complicated members aided in making possible the most rapid delivery and erection of steel tonnage in the history of New York."

Everything in the stripped-down façade was designed to keep costs down. The architects were concerned that a façade containing 6,400 windows would be monotonous, and look more like a perforated shell. Their solution was to make the windows flush with the limestone skin, eliminating deep reveals and their shadows. The brick walls are faced in fine gray Salem limestone from Indiana, "as uniform in color and texture as bread," in the words of the naturalist writer Scott Russell Sanders. The stone is supported directly on the spandrel beams, which eliminated the need for time-consuming angles and brackets. Even the flashy chrome and nickel mullions that run the length of the shaft like vertical railroad tracks could be applied without external scaffolding, and handily covered the joins between the windows, spandrels, and limestone, reducing the finish work.

But we do not love buildings because they are efficient; we love them because they make us dream. Part of the Empire State Building's allure is that it reigned so long unchallenged—42 years—as the world's tallest building, into the age of jet travel and moon landings. The observatory is visited by 3.5 million people annually and was an important source of revenue during the lean rental years of the Great Depression, when it was known as the "Empty State Building." The building did not turn a profit from its leases until 1950.

The Empire State Building is an intensely romantic, even foolish, building. The films *King Kong* and *An Affair to Remember* are as much a part of its lore as its construction ("It's the nearest thing we have to heaven in New York!" Deborah Kerr tells Cary Grant). Improbably, the 16-story, 200-foot, hypodermic-shaped spire with wing-like buttresses was planned as a mooring mast for zeppelins. High winds made the idea completely unfeasible, and in fact the designers had so little grasp of the logistics involved that they showed passengers disembarking from the nose of a docked blimp rather than from the gondola below it.

Romance is what still draws the public: the mighty eagles flanking the Fifth Avenue entry, the imperial lobby lined in richly veined purple and gray German marble, and the streamlined, Moderne canopies above the side-street entrances. Visitors come here to experience architecture, with the same sense of purpose and wonder with which one enters a Gothic cathedral. The setback skyscraper form itself is celebrated everywhere: in the capitals of the limestone pilasters outside, in the elevator door panels, and in the odd little Moderne corbels that support the metal pedestrian bridges in the double-story lobby. The building's top was first floodlit in white in 1964 to mark the World's Fair, and in color for the 1976 National Democratic Convention. Nearly three dozen couples marry here every Valentine's Day in a group wedding.

5

6

[1] The final sequence of KING KONG (1933), atop the Empire State Building, is now folklore. [2] The mast, without the TV antenna added in 1950, is a paean to flight. [3] The limestone façade helps prevent the structure from bending in the wind. [4] The Empire State's archetypal silhouette is unmistakable. [5] A playing card shows the Empire State emitting a beacon of light. [6] Cost-cutting considerations gave the Empire State a stark purity of line.

Waldorf-Astoria Hotel

301 PARK AVENUE » SCHULTZE & WEAVER, 1931

W HEN THE German film director Fritz Lang arrived in New York Harbor in 1924, he was spellbound by the verticality of the city's skyscrapers. These were eclectic buildings such as the Gothic Woolworth Building and the needle-like Beaux-Arts Singer Tower (since demolished), but in his mind's eye, Lang transformed them into a city of modernistic towers. "I looked into the streets—the glaring lights and the tall buildings—and there I conceived *Metropolis,*" Lang recalled. (This story is now considered to be a bit of a Hollywood-type hyperbole, because Lang had the title and concept of the film before then, but the city's influence on the set design cannot be discounted.) "I roamed the streets all day. The buildings struck me as a vertical curtain, glistening and very light, an opulent stage backdrop hung against a gloomy sky to dazzle, to distract, and to hypnotize."

Lang returned to Berlin, and two years later completed his visionary silent classic, whose futuristic cityscapes in turn influenced a generation of American architects. The sets of

Metropolis, designed by Otto Hunte, Erich Kettelhut, and Karl Vollbrecht, used 500 scale-model skyscrapers to create a multitiered city of aerial causeways, massive, close-set towers and monstrous boulevards. The finned turrets of the Waldorf-Astoria bear more than a passing resemblance to the crown of the central tower in *Metropolis.*

The contract for this 29-story, $42-million hotel that replaced the original Astor Hotel, a white elephant that was demolished to make way for the Empire State Building, was signed on the day of the stock market crash, October 29, 1929. Eighty percent of the site, which takes up the entire block between Park and Lexington Avenues and East 48th and East 49th Streets, is supported on steel pylons over the tracks of the New York Central Railroad. A separate elevator once shunted guests directly from their private railroad cars, in a modernist fantasy of unlimited transportation.

The Waldorf was conceived as a city under one roof. A contemporaneous axonometric view through the hotel shows a cross section of 2,200

rooms, ballrooms, bars, shops, and kitchens (the blind, third-floor façade behind the hotel's name in raised, gilded letters conceals a block-long kitchen). The triple-story ballroom was the largest in the world when it was built, and the combined ballrooms could fit 6,000 guests. Herbert Hoover and Douglas MacArthur lived their last years in the Waldorf Towers, where every president since Hoover has stayed. The ground-floor parking garage below the towers was built to accommodate the turning radius of a Rolls-Royce Corniche.

The Waldorf is a seamless synthesis of modern classical and Expressionist styles. Its stark, 17-story limestone wings with crenellated parapets and verdigris copper turrets reflect Expressionism's Gothic roots. The zigzag motifs of the turrets resemble the crisp modern classicism of the urns atop Joseph Urban's Hearst Magazine Building. The extraordinary, windowless, block-through lobby, with its dark panels of Oregon maple and black granite pilasters, creates a hidden Expressionist grotto, but the effect is softened by light-hearted French Deco bas-reliefs of pipers, dancers, actors, leaping antelope, and frozen fountains.

[1] Vintage cars line Park Avenue outside the main entrance.   [2] The Waldorf is a city under one roof with the appurtenances of a luxury liner.   [3] The turrets seem to have sprung from the imaginations of German Expressionist set designers.

McGraw-Hill Building

F O R   T H E I R watershed 1932 exhibition at the newly founded Museum of Modern Art, "The International Style: Architecture Since 1922," Henry-Russell Hitchcock and Philip Johnson chose only one New York City skyscraper: Raymond Hood's McGraw-Hill Building. "The lightness, simplicity and lack of applied verticalism marks this skyscraper as an advance over other New York skyscrapers and bring it within the limits of the International Style," the critics wrote. "The setbacks are handled more frankly than in other skyscrapers, though still reminiscent of the pyramidal shape of traditional towers." However, they faulted Hood's billboard top: "the heavy ornamental crown is an illogical and unhappy break in the general system of regularity and weights down the whole design." Of course, in the postmodern era, the sign with 11-foot-high letters that spell out the company's name is one of the building's most welcome aspects.

The McGraw-Hill is anomalous in that Hood fused the severe International Style with the commercial New York setback style, and even more strikingly colored the whole in sea green. In a 1927 forum on "modernistic views on color schemes in skyscrapers," Hood predicted that entire skyscrapers "will eventually have a distinct color. To color only the architectural embellishments and a few outstanding cornices and façades will appear like the rose decorations on a woman's white dress. They are hardly noticeable. It is best for the whole building to be of one color. . . . New York of the future, I believe, will consist of gaily colored buildings." Almost no one took up Hood's challenge until the postmodern era, when entire buildings were covered in rose granite.

In the McGraw-Hill, continuous bands of green-metal-framed windows alternate with panels of turquoise terra-cotta blocks. The publisher James McGraw called the color "perfectly awful" and said he must have been ill the day he chose it (curiously, the McGraw-Hill's color resembles Babylon's Ishtar Gate). The McGraw-Hill was terra cotta's last gasp; it was increasingly seen as an old-fashioned material by the Internationalists, who preferred to build with the industrial materials of steel, concrete, and glass.

The 35-story, 480-foot McGraw-Hill reveals Hood's plastic as opposed to pictorial sense of architecture; it's really a setback tower elongated into slab form. The result looks as if was cut with a palette knife out of blocks of green plasticene, an effect enhanced by the brutally plain cornices of the setbacks. The plan of the building is quite utilitarian: the broad platform housed the printing plant for the publisher, the slab was for office space, and the fanciful crown for executive offices. The streamlined, opaque glass panels of the Moderne lobby are an ornamental departure, resembling a deck of a luxury ocean liner. The tiered Deco crown, seen from the east or west, also looks like the superstructure of a giant liner.

Rem Koolhaas has the last word on Hood's jukebox modernism: "Once again Hood has combined two incompatibles in a single whole; its golden shades pulled down to reflect the sun, the McGraw-Hill Building looks like a fire raging inside an iceberg: the fire of Manhattanism inside the iceberg of modernism."

[1] A literal representation of the skyscraper as a tiered layer cake.   [2] A 1931 company newsletter details the logistics of the move.   [3] The original 11-story McGraw Publishing Building in 1907.   [4] The Hill Building in 1914; the two companies merged in 1917.

General Electric Building

(originally RCA Victor Building)   570 LEXINGTON AVENUE » CROSS & CROSS, 1931

DESIGNED AS the headquarters for the RCA Victor Company—but taken over only a year later by General Electric and known ever since as the GE Building—this slender, orange-brick tower is one of the most extravagantly Expressionist buildings in New York. Gothic and German Expressionist motifs are brilliantly overlaid in this 40-story, 570-foot-tall tower. The result is nothing less than a secular cathedral devoted to the gods of radio.

The spire is an extraordinary image of the romantic aspirations of American businessmen as the country entered the Depression. The RCA Victor Building in particular seems to have been built with a higher purpose in mind—to celebrate the new medium of radio. The diamond-shape motifs in the façade have a dual meaning, signifying the piezoelectric crystal by which old radios operated, and the stylus that produced sound from records. The marvelous terra-cotta spandrels in rose, ochre, and verdigris can be interpreted as a radio dial, or a needle in the grooves of a record. At the rounded corner of the 12-story platform, a scrolled musical instrument symbolizes RCA's recording business. The building's theme may have been inspired by early crystal radios, also known as cathedral radios because of the Gothic styling of their wooden cabinets.

Strange, mummified-looking figures occupy different levels of the façade. These are the Tiki gods of radio. One fills a niche at street level, like the figure of a saint. Crackling energy fields radiate from behind four grim-faced, double-story-tall figures in the crown, with haloed heads grouped at their feet. Are these disciples? The enlightened radio audience? It is hard to believe now that American business ever reached this dizzy pinnacle of Expressionism. The intersecting, gilded radio waves in the crown are fused with the openwork tracery of a Gothic cathedral, revealing the Gothic roots of Expressionism in a breathtaking syncretic image. Gilded bolts of energy aimed heavenward replace the finials of a Gothic spire.

In the same way that the multitudinous heavenward-pointing layers of a Gothic cathedral suggested the City of Heaven, the cornices of the GE Building are themselves miniature images of the skyline. The setback form is reified everywhere—at the base of columns, in the window casings and in the miniature symbolic buttresses above the corner clock.

If skeptics think this is an overinterpretation, read what the architect John W. Cross himself wrote about the barrel-vaulted, aluminum-colored lobby ceiling:

Romantic though radio may be, it is at the same time intangible and elusive—a thing which can be captured visually only through symbolism.... The severity of the vertical lines which intersect the curves of the ceiling with daring abruptness is intended to convey the directness and penetration of radio itself.

The building materials are sumptuous: a base of rose granite, entries and windows framed in toothsome orange marble, salmon-colored glazed brick, and polychromatic terra cotta highlighted with gilding. The crown fairly sings in the morning light. The building was also contextual before there was a word for it; it was meant to harmonize in color and spatial arrangement with the dome of St. Bart's at its foot on Park Avenue. On cannot help but think that the composition of spire and dome influenced the Trylon and Perisphere of the World's Fair of 1939.

[1]   A scrolling musical instrument represents RCA's recording interests.   [2] Lavish attention was devoted to the brickwork and terra-cotta detailing.

City Bank Farmers Trust Company Building

22 WILLIAM STREET » CROSS & CROSS, 1931

FAR BE it from architects to admit they are doing anything other than designing the most practical building for its site. "The design of a modern skyscraper is not primarily a matter of aesthetic expression," Cross & Cross wrote, presumably with faces as straight as the bizarre, heroically scaled heads that gaze down from their City Bank Farmers Trust Company Building. The parti of the building—with a blunt, slender, chamfered tower torqued against a keystone-shaped 15-story platform—was a response to factors such as the irregular site, the need to accommodate 5,000 bank employees and 2,000 additional renters, zoning laws, the intervals of elevator service, and the height at which the building would make a profitable return. But that goes little towards explaining the

tower's extraordinary mix of Neo-Renaissance, Expressionist, and modern classical styles.

Bankers tend to be more conservative than communications and entertainment people, so Cross & Cross toned down the extravagant Expressionism of their earlier RCA Victor Building for the 57-story, 685-foot, ⅞-inch-tall tower. With its combination of rich materials and historicist detailing, the Neo-Renaissance style bespoke wealth and tradition, an image the bank certainly wished to convey. But a bank also needs to look up to date, so there is an overlay of modern classical styling.

The strangely ambitious scale of the building gives it an Expressionist quality. Giant coins of foreign nations with strong agricultural and mining interests (including Cuba) frame the semicircular arched entryway, representing the bank's foreign investments. The pierced stone spandrels, which do double duty as air intakes, are decorated with agricultural motifs—flower heads, sheaves of wheat, hour glasses (for investment), balancing scales (for trade), eagles and fasces (for the role of government). The building is sheathed in sand-colored Alabama Rockwood limestone, with (now very sooty) white-brick piers, spandrels, and mullions in the tower, interspersed with stone beltcourses. The buttresses that resemble sentinels at the first setback show an Art Moderne influence in their streamlined Greek helmets, and are said to represent "giants of finance." Perhaps disingenuously, Cross & Cross insisted that even these Easter Island heads on the building were functional because they "serve as a concealment for the exhaust vents which are conducted through their backs to invisible louvered outlets."

The interiors are sheer luxe, meant to show off the bank's prestige, with a stenciled silver-and-gray rotunda inside the William Street entrance. With its indirect lighting, the rotunda creates an Expressionist grotto. The main lobby is floored in golden travertine and polychrome Cosmatesque marble with a base of rouge

Examples of the beautiful grille work and metal castings done in bronze and nickel, which decorate window guards and ventilators in the new building

2

3

antique, a surbase of red altico marble, door enframents, pilaster columns, and stair treads in rosato d'or with rouge antique risers and walls of Vaurian stone.

Gorgeously wrought, nickel-silver-alloy, bas-relief doors and grilles by the sculptor David Evans depict classically garbed figures representing Architecture, Engineering, Mechanics, and Navigation.

1

[1] The symbols, clockwise from top left, are Architecture, Engineering, Mechanics, and Navigation.   [2] One Wall Street's slender shaft evokes the romantic self-image of American business.   [3] Easter Island–like stone heads guard ventilation grilles in the façade.

Cities Service Building

(now 70 Pine Street)

CLINTON & RUSSELL, 1932

THE SLENDER, 67-story spire of 70 Pine Street, the last skyscraper built in financial district during the Depression, is one of the most extravagantly Expressionist. It is an eerie snapshot of the stone skyscraper evolving into glass architecture. The limestone-sheathed shaft, so narrow that double elevators had to be used to service all the floors, supports a faceted-glass pinnacle, illuminated from within, in fulfillment of the visionary writings of Bruno Taut, Paul Scheerbart, and other German Expressionist architects. Glass architecture existed more on paper than in reality, because there was no major construction in Germany between the wars. In his trance-like essay of 1914, "Glass Architecture," Scheerbart wrote that society can be transformed only "if we take away the closed character from the rooms in which we live. We can only do that by introducing glass architecture, which lets in the light of the sun, the moon, and the stars, not merely through a few windows, but through every possible wall, which will be made entirely of glass—colored glass."

Scheerbart's prediction was almost right, except that it was the office building more than the home that would be transformed. His vision of glass architecture was a bit of an evolutionary dead-end, because by the time construction resumed in the postwar boom, Expressionism was considered wholly outdated, and was replaced by the pure geometry of Internationalism. The Flash Gordon–like green glowing jewel atop 70 Pine Street is almost sui generis. However, postmodern architects such as Cesar Pelli in the World Financial Center, and David Childs of Skidmore, Owings & Merrill in the Worldwide Plaza celebrate 70 Pine's parti of stone metamorphosing into glass.

Strangely, for a group that sought to break with the past, the Expressionists held up the unified artistry of the Gothic cathedral as an ideal. The Cities Service Building has a charming, syncretic image at its entry, where a model of the skyscraper stands between the two portals, in the space reserved for a saint in a Gothic cathedral. The observation platform (now closed), not much bigger than a helicopter bubble, features a brilliant coup de theatre: the tiny, five-passenger elevator rises up through the floor like a sidewalk elevator, and then retracts to provide untrammeled 360-degree views of the city. The leather-paneled conference room on the floor below is no longer in use.

[1] A dramatic night view of the crown.   [2] A model of the building occupies a place above the doors usually reserved for a saint.

One Wall Street

(originally Irving Trust Company Building)

RALPH WALKER, 1932

LIKE DYING pharaohs, Wall Street bankers built extraordinary monuments to themselves in the wake of the 1929 stock market crash. One Wall, with its 50-story, 654-foot-tall white limestone towers, is one of the most delicate, even feminine, skyscrapers ever built. Fluted walls, faceted windows, and chamfered corners give the tower a mineral grace, like folds of cloth sculpted in stone. The 180-by-110-foot site without improvements was assessed at $10,250,000—or $520 a square foot—a fortune in Depression dollars.

This building is the acme of Expressionist and modern classical styles in New York, from the triple-story faceted windows of the observation lounge that loom like the rookery of some great Gothic flying creature, to the richly mosaiced first-floor banking hall that glitters like a hall in tsarist Russia. Here, Wall Street's captains unabashedly gave themselves over to the romance of American business, even while other Americans stood in soup lines. Softly luminescent kappa shells once adorned the observation lounge's faceted ceiling. The walls were decorated with motifs of Native American war bonnets, an interesting choice since Wall Street is so named because of a wall that protected Dutch settlers from the Munsee Indians.

Best known for his vertically treated yet massive brick buildings for the New York Telephone Company, Walker pulled out all the stops in making the Irving Trust a luxury tower. The delicately incised, fluted shaft rises straight from the sidewalk for 20 stories, before beginning a series of subtle transitions to the astylar crown, with its deeply punched windows. Depending on the light and angle from which it is seen, the tower resembles folds of cloth draped sinuously from a frame, or a natural, cliff-like object. Walker was moving away from the Internationalist view that the exterior of a building should reflect nothing more than its interior spaces. He later wrote, "once you admit . . . that the bones need a skin to protect the interior, then the skin becomes a matter of whatever ardent experience that man can bring forth to create delight as well as strength."

The main banking room, decorated by the mosaicist Hildreth Meier, is nothing but delightful. Its tent-like walls appear to be folds of rich brocade hanging from the ceiling. The sumptuous chamber looks back to the lushness and naturalistic motifs of Art Nouveau rather than the machine aesthetic of modern classicism. The coloration is gorgeous, shading from red tiles against a blue setting to brilliant orange against black in the ceiling, above a red terrazzo floor and a burgundy dado. Veins of gold tile flash amidst the colors, reflecting torchières that turn the space into an intimate grotto. At night, seen through the deeply faceted street-level windows, the chamber glows like a fairyland of riches.

[1] Trinity Church's steeple, right, was once the highest point in Manhattan.

Metropolitan Life Insurance Company, North Building

11–25 MADISON AVENUE » HARVEY WILEY CORBETT AND D. EVERETT WAID, 1932

DESIGNED TO be the tallest building in the world, the uncompleted Metropolitan Life North Building stands like a tombstone for the skyscraper boom of the 1920s. Other than the privately financed Rockefeller Center, no new tall buildings went up until after the war. The nature of those buildings, too, would change, because American businessmen were no longer interested in romantic monuments to themselves, but instead were eyeing the bottom line.

Originally meant to be the base for an 80- to 100-story tower, the building topped out at 28 stories because the Depression intervened. There is some question whether Met Life seriously intended to complete the tower, but the platform is still built to scale for a much larger building. What's left is a hulking, limestone-sheathed base. The scale is gigantic, from the oversized domed loggia entrances at the four corners to the banks of 30 elevators that service almost as many floors—absolutely no waiting in this building. The oversized round-headed arched entryways in the middle of East 24th Street could have served as the inspiration for Philip Johnson's theatrically scaled AT&T Building (now the Sony Building). The bow-shaped base, strongly indebted to Ralph Walker's designs with its jagged, faceted corners, would have made a striking foil for the astylar shaft.

Inside, the grand lobby is Neo-Renaissance styled, with a coffered, silver-leaf ceiling above gold-veined walls in Italian cremo marble and floors of pink Tennessee granite. Bas-reliefs present the ideals of the insurance company, with allegorical figures of Recreation, Health, Thrift, Security, and Industry. In the era before computers, two lower floors were designed with ceilings less than seven feet high, to hold filing cabinets in a space that covers an entire city block. When the First Boston investment bank leased the building in 1994, they punched through the two floors to create a 15-foot high trading floor for their investment bankers. A pedestrian bridge, beloved by the Expressionists, connects the North and South

buildings. The building was designed for Met Life employees. At its peak in the 1960s, the company employed 25,000 people. The connecting buildings were constructed in four stages over a ten-year period.

The design by Harvey Wiley Corbett and D. Everett Waid was forward-looking not only because of its telescoping shape (the Lipstick Building is a distant relative) but also because it would have used triangular metal and glass bays, even though the city building code required masonry construction. The overall design bore a strong resemblance to Hugh Ferriss's renderings for crystalline towers sheathed in glass. In his 1929 book *Metropolis of Tomorrow*, Ferriss often sounded like he was taking shorthand from another dimension:

> *Buildings like crystals.*
> *Walls of translucent glass.*
> *Sheer glass blocks sheathing a steel grill.*
> *No Gothic branch: no Acanthus leaf: no*
> *   recollection of the plant world.*
> *A mineral kingdom.*
> *Gleaming stalagmites.*
> *Forms as cold as ice.*
> *Mathematics.*
> *Night in the Science Zone.*

Ferriss presciently noted, "The new types of glass, which modern ingenuity is already manufacturing, make it quite certain that before long this material will be utilized not simply as windows but as walls."

The North Building is a forerunner of the giant floor plates that characterize postwar office buildings. The floors of the base are 80 feet deep, made possible by the use of full air-conditioning and by indirect lighting to supplement natural lighting from the windows. Employees worked in enormous, communal spaces, later made famous as a symbol of modern impersonality in the 1960 film *The Apartment*, which used the actual Met Life steno pool.

DIRECTIONS *Cut dotted line with scissors; picture puzzle will fall apart, then see how quickly you can put the picture together again.* PATENT APPLIED FOR.

1

[1] The tower replaced Stanford White's exquisite Madison Square Presbyterian Church (1906). center.

Rockefeller Center

WEST 48TH TO WEST 51ST STREETS, BETWEEN FIFTH AND SIXTH AVENUES »
RAYMOND HOOD; CORBETT, HARRISON & MACMURRAY;
GODLEY & FOULIHOUX; REINHARD & HOFMEISTER, 1932–40

1

ROCKEFELLER CENTER is at once a summa of the Art Deco style, and a look ahead to the Internationalist style that dominated after World War II. Financed privately by the Rockefeller fortune at a time when America's banks failed, Rockefeller Center was the last major construction in the city until ground was broken for the United Nations in 1947. Other than the World's Fair of 1939, which consisted largely of temporary buildings, Rockefeller Center was the most grandiloquent statement of the ideals of Depression-era America.

The Rockefellers actually hired a consulting philosopher, Hartley Burr Alexander of the University of Southern California, to come up with a "theme for Rockefeller City." Alexander saw in the complex the image of "Homo Fabor—Man the Builder," as well as capitalism's "answer to the Bolshevist challenge." After a couple of rewrites, the center's theme was changed to the March of Civilization, but not before some of the major artworks had been commissioned.

Though a remarkably unified urban complex, Rockefeller Center originated as a proposal for a new home for the Metropolitan Opera, then evolved into a headquarters, television studio, and entertainment complex for the RCA and General Electric companies. John D. Rockefeller and his right-hand man John R. Todd developed the site to profit from the leases. Rarely has a private enterprise given itself over so extravagantly to public space and works of art. The plaza and its celebrated skating rink developed serendipitously in the early 1940s: a holdover from the opera plan, the below-street-level plaza was planned as a grand connection to the subway, but the subway line was not completed in time for the opening of the plaza. The developers found themselves with an expensive hole in the ground. They tried luxe shops and cafés, with little public response. Someone

suggested a roller rink, but that only brought in young toughs from nearby Hell's Kitchen. Finally someone thought of figure skating, an upper-class pursuit in the Depression, and the result looks as if it was always meant to be.

As the dominant architect, Hood's designs for the center were in many ways a culmination of the modernist ideal city. Hood in fact was a champion of the skyscraper's culture of congestion that Rem Koolhaas writes about. "Congestion is good," Hood affirmed, "it's the best thing we have in New York. The glory of the skyscraper is that we have provided for it so well." The buildings were designed to be connected by rooftop causeways, but these were abandoned because of cost and liability considerations. With the center's rooftop gardens, Hood straddled both the romance of Art Deco and the orthodoxy of Internationalism, evoking in his words the "fabled living tapestry of the hanging gardens of Babylon" on one hand, and Le Corbusier's Plan Voisin (1925), with its pristine towers set amid verdant gardens, on the other.

Le Corbusier did not return the compliment. He arrived in New York in 1933, peering through his owlish spectacles, puffing on a *mégot* and sneering that "The trouble with New York is that its skyscrapers are too small. And there are too many of them." The RCA Building was good, he said, but declared that the George Washington Bridge was the "only seat of grace in a disordered city." Le Corbusier's comment was prescient, because the bare-bones exposed-steel architecture of the bridge helped bring about public acceptance of the Internationalist aesthetic of pure structure over ornamentation.

The 70-story, 850-foot-tall, limestone-clad RCA Building (now the GE Building at 30 Rock) was the last great Deco tower built in New York, although it is also fused with the postwar Internationalist slab form. In an even more dramatic progression of his thinking from

[1] Lee Lawrie's ATLAS was part of an ambitious program of public art.

1

2

3

the McGraw-Hill Building, Hood exaggerated the slab and tower features to extremes. Seen head on, the tower, which narrows progressively with each setback, dematerializes into the clouds like a Gothic cathedral. But from the side, the tower appears as a monumental, block-long slab, brought down to human scale by its low, projecting wings that continue the traditional cornice line of the street.

Hood, who died at 53 in 1934 without living to see the completion of the project, accomplished something radically new by setting the modernist object of the RCA Building within the classical Beaux-Arts symmetry of the surrounding buildings. The RCA is modernist because it requires a viewer to complete the picture; there is no one single image of the building. Setting such an unstable object within the complex's static symmetry makes the whole space vibrate and flow with a modernist sense of energy, much like the figure-ground effects of the shallow-setbacked tower against the broad sky. The symmetrically balanced outer buildings are set in a pinwheel pattern around the axis of the RCA Building, lending dynamism to a classically ordered setting.

The imagery behind the RCA can be interpreted as a the frozen cascades of a fountain. In *The Skyward Trend of Thought*, Thomas A. P. van Leeuwen writes of the RCA that the "slab is cascading downwards, and like the waters of a fountain, is ending its voyage in the basin at the foot of the tower. Then the waters are sent up again in order to demonstrate in detail the principles of the largest frozen fountain ever built . . . as it is usually frozen and used as a skating rink (the Energy Bringing Prometheus riding on its crest makes it into a classic case of symbolism redundant)."

The center's artwork was developed as if it was to be looked back on by future archaeologists. The French and English Buildings are laid out like the arms of a sphinx in front of the RCA Building. After traveling to Europe to enlist the services of Henri Matisse and Pablo Picasso, Hood signed up José Maria Sert and the socialist artist Diego Rivera, who played a trick on old John D. Jr. by painting a mural of Lenin in the stronghold of capitalism. Sert painted the monochrome lobby mural inside the RCA Building depicting America as the pinnacle of progress, with a *stadtkröne* of the RCA Building

in the background. In his book *Rockefeller Center: Architecture as Theater*, the critic Alan Balfour noted that the mural's spiraling airplanes were meant to suggest man's conquest of time and space, but also ominously foretold the coming war in Europe.

As the headquarters of NBC, the building abounds with arcane symbols of broadcasting. Some of the images are baffling even with a key: Barry Faulkner's mosaic above the entry to the former American Metal Climax Building (a name that could have been conjured up by William S. Burroughs) shows Thought, who—through the medium of radio waves and her agents Publicity and Hygiene—delivers the Working Stiff (represented in a dingy tank top) from the demons of Poverty and Ignorance (and—presumably—Grayish Laundry). Above the West 51st Street side, a woman representing Transmission waves her hand over a line of dancers, which are picked up in miniature by the matched figure of Reception, watched by Mother Earth, and her child, Man.

[1] The roof gardens realize the modernist fantasy of a multitiered city.   [2] Watching people work was something of a spectator sport in the Great Depression.   [3] Diego Rivera and Frida Kahlo discuss his mural, which was ultimately rejected because it featured Lenin.   [4] Workmen receive their pay in front of Rockefeller Center's first Christmas tree on December 24, 1931.   [5] Originally designed as a subway entrance, the plaza eventually became the celebrated skating rink.   [6] Atlas shrugged: craftsmen put finishing touches on the statue of Atlas.

100 Park Avenue

THE FIRST large office building constructed in New York after the Depression, 100 Park Avenue is astylar in a way that the prewar modernists did not imagine. The squat, unlovely building is almost without style, little more than the product of the office space contained within in conformance with the zoning code on the outside, but it is an important forerunner of the postwar skyscraper.

Two significant technological advances distinguish 100 Park. With the advent of central air-conditioning and fluorescent lighting, buildings no longer needed to be responsive to the environment. The big office building now manufactured its own weather and diurnal systems, truly a city within a city.

Much of Art Deco design was predicated on the fact that offices could be no more than 27 or 28 feet deep for adequate access to air and light, in order to command premium rentals. The Empire State, the Daily News, and the RCA Buildings owe much of their parti to a calculation of desirable office space grouped around elevator cores. The Metropolitan Life North Building, with its squat, hulking silhouette and 80-foot-deep floor plates, presaged the shape of things to come in the form of 100 Park Avenue.

The emphasis of the postwar office building was no longer on height or dramatic silhouettes, but on sheer, burgeoning floor space. Known as a "block-through" building because it takes up the entire front of a city block, 100 Park is only 36 floors tall, but contains 825,815 square feet of space. The ground floor alone is 40,000 square feet, taking up the full 200-foot block between Park and Madison Avenues, with a 240-foot front on East 40th Street and a 146-foot front on East 41st Street. With columns set 15 to 21 feet apart, the floor space is open and flexible, ready to be subdivided with cubicles to meet the tenant's needs. In the period from 1940 to 1960, the number of white-collar workers doubled,

and there was a commensurate growth in office space. Postwar corporations liked to consolidate their operations on one floor.

With its flat-topped white-brick piers, the building was almost devoid of ornament (a recent renovation introduced some Greek-diner-style retro detailing). The Park Avenue façade, organized into nine bays of four windows with metal spandrels and protruding stainless steel mullions, conforms mechanically to the zoning code. The bulky platform rises 13 stories, sets back for two stories like a break in a trouser crease, and culminates in a broad shaft, capped with a blunt utility tower. The clipped, grid-like design looks as if it had sprung directly off the drafting board, and still bore the ferrule marks.

In 1950, Lee Thompson Smith, president of the Real Estate Board of New York, wrote:

These buildings are modern. Primarily because they are air-conditioned. But one salient characteristic of the new buildings that cannot be adapted to old buildings at any price is their basic planning. They provide large blocks of space on one floor, with great glass areas, better lighting, fewer courts, less waste space, and new automatic elevator arrangements, with fewer cars and faster service. Deeper floor areas, among the other developments in design, result in as much as eighty percent of the space on each floor being rentable space, as compared with sixty-five percent in the buildings that were conventional twenty years ago.

[1] 100 Park Avenue was the prototype of the block-through office building.   [2] Ely Jacques Kahn, second from left, points out the advantages of his boxy design.

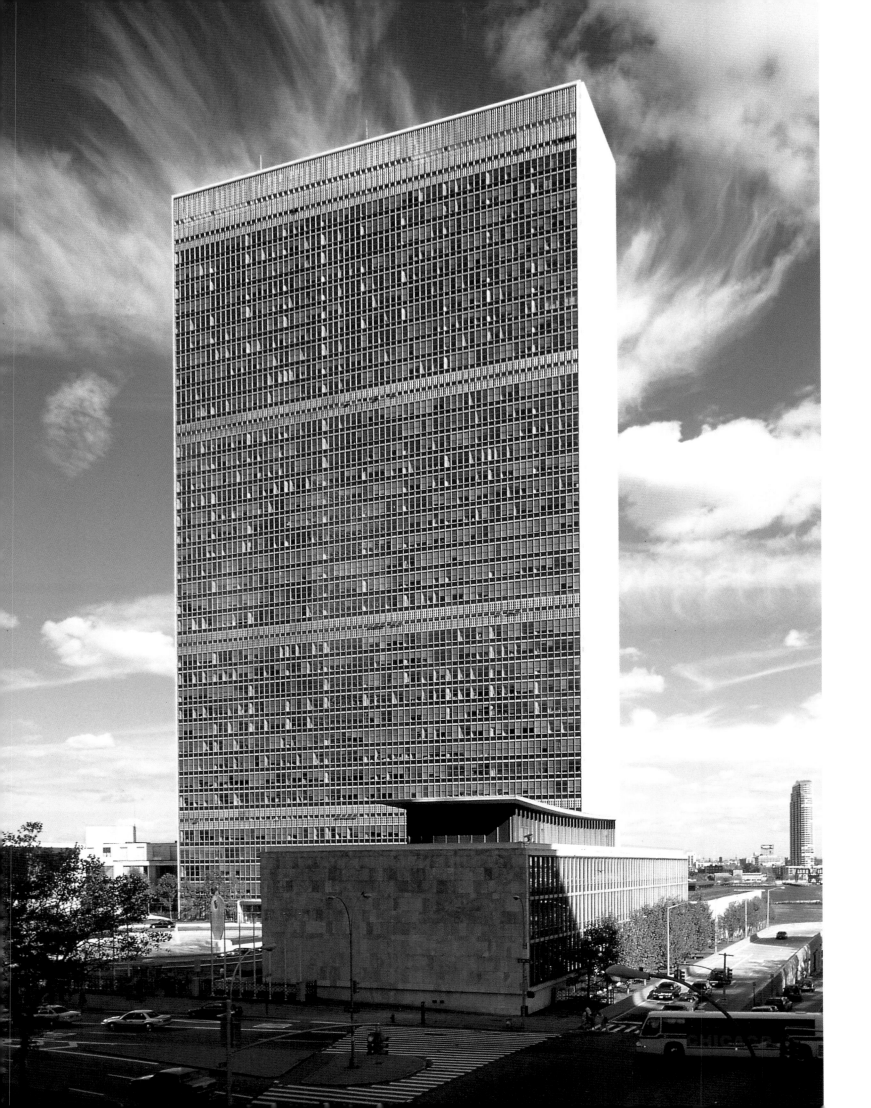

United Nations Secretariat

FIRST AVENUE BETWEEN EAST 42ND AND EAST 48TH STREETS »

INTERNATIONAL COMMITTEE OF ARCHITECTS, WALLACE K. HARRISON, CHAIRMAN, 1947–53

1

THE 39-STORY, 544-foot-high, 287-foot-wide United Nations Secretariat, the first glass curtain-wall slab in New York, became the visual symbol of postwar architecture throughout the world. Americans and Europeans were eager to adopt Internationalism as the start of a new era, untainted by associations with the past, specifically the carnage of World War II.

The design of the complex originated in the World's Fairs, dating back to the unified aesthetic of the White City in the World's Columbian Exposition of 1893, fused with Le Corbusier's Ville Radieuse ideal of towers in a garden. The American leader of the design board, Wallace K. Harrison, had designed the emblematic Trylon and Perisphere for the 1939 World's Fair, and was searching for similar Platonic forms to set on a greensward. Le Corbusier seized upon the Secretariat tower as his personal mission. The rest of the team, largely undistinguished except for Oscar Niemeyer of Brazil, were selected according to global political spheres. Mies van der Rohe and Walter Gropius were omitted because they were associated with the defeated enemy, Germany,

and Alvar Aalto was left out because Finland was not yet a UN member. Frank Lloyd Wright, never much of a team player, was not seriously considered.

The proposed site for the headquarters was the grounds of the 1939 World's Fair in Flushing Meadow Park, Queens, for which a number of the UN architects had designed the pavilions for their countries, another thematic link between the projects. The UN plan was launched when the Rockefeller family bought up and donated 17 acres of the old slaughterhouse district along the East River, bordered by First Avenue between East 41st and East 47th Streets for $8.5 million in December 1946. Wallace Harrison had also worked as a junior design member for Rockefeller Center, and the decorative schemes for both projects bear remarkable similarities.

The immediate focus of interest was the skyscraper of the Secretariat Building. As Harrison put it, "Nobody talked about the Assembly, the center of the whole thing; each architect wanted to do the office building because the European architects had never built a tower and they couldn't resist that opportunity!" Arguments over the complex were as rancorous as a cold war Security Council meeting. Le Corbusier, the great Swiss rationalist, behaved like an enfant terrible: He once ripped all the sketches off the boardroom walls except for his own, and leaked a rendering of his design without the board's approval to the *New York Herald Tribune* on May 22, 1947.

The plan went through many permutations. At one stage, the Secretariat was located at the plaza's north end, and Robert Moses, the czar-like City Construction Coordinator went ahead and widened 47th Street, even though the building was finally placed on 44th Street. Le Corbusier's Project 23A, as it is called, was a close approximation of the final plan, with the

[1] the focus of the plaza is on the Secretariat rather than the General Assembly. foreground.   [2] The esplanade and Conference Building were cantilevered over the FDR Drive along the East River.

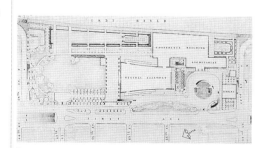

2

slab of the Secretariat piercing the low horizontal block of the combined General Assembly and Conference buildings. Oscar Niemeyer, Le Corbusier's disciple and former employee, came up with Project 23W, the synthesis that was ultimately adopted, in which the General Assembly was reduced in scale and moved to the north of the Secretariat to create a park with buildings.

The slab form of the Secretariat, with glass curtain walls bookended by 72-foot-deep walls of white Vermont marble is an evolution of Le Corbusier's solid-edged slabs of the Pavillon Suisse (1932) in Paris and his Ministry of Education and Health Building with Oscar Niemeyer in Rio de Janeiro (1938). There were still battles to be fought: Le Corbusier wanted windows that opened and were protected by an awning-like *brise-soleil* as a natural means of climate control. Harrison insisted that air-conditioning was the cornerstone of the Pax Americana, and designed an innovative curtain

wall cantilevered two feet, nine inches, in front of the steel structure so that it formed a flush skin of blue-green Thermopane heat-absorbing glass. The Thermopane spandrels between the window bands were painted black on the inner face. With French invective, Le Corbusier dismissed this "cellophane veil" as "sepulchral repression." Nonetheless, the slab was a crisp précis of the Internationalist aesthetic and set the pace for glass curtain-wall buildings in New York and around the world. For Americans, Internationalism represented postwar prosperity; for Europe it was a chance to rebuild; and for developing countries it stood for a brighter future.

The interior of the five-story, curvilinear General Assembly at the foot of the Secretariat is a museum of modernism, circa 1947, preserved like an insect in amber. Boomerang-shaped, cantilevered balconies dominate the open lobby, below a ceiling of exposed air ducts. A gray-and-white checkerboard terrazzo paving sweeps

under plate-glass walls, interspersed with exposed steel I beam columns. The period details are perfect: flying stairways with planters below them, recessed "cheese-hole" ceiling lights, brushed aluminum bullet lamps, cherry-wood paneling, and turquoise leather banquettes. The overtly allegorical representational artwork is very much in the Rockefeller Center model, with murals culminating in the construction of the UN itself, and optimistic visions of the world to come.

The Internationalists sought to stamp out history rather than build upon it. The superblock plaza of the UN is steeped in the antiurbanism of Internationalism, but the complex works so well precisely because it is supposed to be a separate zone, in fact not even a part of the United States. Built out over the FDR Drive, the plaza looks more like an aircraft carrier moored along the East River than part of the city's fabric. As a symbol of the UN, the complex oddly glorifies its bureaucracy by making the offices of the 14,000 international civil servants its focus, rather than the General Assembly, which lurks, blind-walled and Nautilus-like, at its foot.

[1] Brave new world: Dag Hammarskjold in front of the Secretariat in 1953.   [2] The UN's sheer glass façade became an icon of the Internationalist Style.

Lever House

GROUND FLOOR   SECOND FLOOR   THIRD FLOOR   0 10 25   50

THE DELICATE, glass-walled Lever House stands on Park Avenue like an outpost of a rarefied, more suburban civilization. At 21 stories and 302 feet tall, it qualifies more as a mini-skyscraper, but it had an extraordinary influence on skyscraper design as one of the earliest and best glass curtain-wall office buildings.

Glass buildings were proposed after World War I by Expressionist architects such as Bruno Taut, who envisioned an Oz-like scenario where "columns and arches of emerald green glass rise up over a sea of clouds on the snowy summit of a high mountain." Ludwig Mies van der Rohe, oddly enough the son of a stone mason, proposed the first glass-walled skyscraper in 1921, before it was quite technically feasible.

Lever House was New Yorkers' first look at an all-glass building. The contrast with the stately stone Rue Corridor of Park Avenue could not have been more startling. One need only look at early photos of the Lever with clunky black automobiles in the foreground to realize that Americans had rarely seen anything so spanking new. All exposed sides are covered with sea-green glass and opaque blue-green glass spandrels superimposed with an aluminum grid (the service core is discreetly hidden behind white brick in the northwest corner). Unlike a lot of modern architecture from that period, the Lever is still bright, minty-fresh, and smacks of prosperity.

"Thin skin was in the air," Gordon Bunshaft, the stocky, buzz-cut, creative force behind Skidmore, Owings & Merrill, said about

the postwar period. He synthesized prevailing ideas in modern architecture: "I owned a lot of books, especially about Le Corbu and Mies, but I never studied them the way some people did," he once recalled. "I have a bad habit, which is a lazy one, of not reading the texts."

From Le Corbusier's Ville de Savoie, Bunshaft took the idea of setting his slabs on *pilotis*, as a statement of pure geometry. As with Mies, the structure is readily apparent to the eye: The slabs are cantilevered out from steel columns and wrapped in a glass skin. Americans rediscovered Frank Lloyd Wright via the Internationalists. With its plaza that sweeps uninterruptedly through the glass-membraned lobby, Lever House looks like a formulation of Wright's blending of interior and exterior space. Perhaps because his ideas had been adopted so completely, Wright carped that Lever House was nothing more than "a box on sticks."

But Lever House is something more: it is a perfect tabletop model of postwar American idealism. Charles Luckman, the head of Lever House who had been trained as an architect, told Bunshaft only that he wanted something new, clean (befitting of a soap company), spectacular, and American. Bunshaft came up with a suburban idyll. With a 63-car underground garage, the Lever was designed so that an executive could drive from the suburbs, park, have lunch in the third-floor company cafeteria, even play a round of shuffleboard on the landscaped second-floor terrace, and go home—all without ever setting foot in the dirty, chaotic city. Lever House was the first sealed, fully climate-controlled building, with fixed windows held in place by aluminum mullions, so that Lever employees did not even breathe the same air as city dwellers. Even the stainless-steel *pilotis* are shod with little black-concrete plinth blocks, as if the building was afraid of getting its feet dirty.

The parti is wildly impractical from a real-estate point of view, and was never copied, although the glass skin was so influential. Three-quarters of the site is occupied by empty air. The 18-story tower contains a relatively scanty 8,700 square feet per floor. The overall floor space is 280,000 square feet, the equivalent of only an eight-story building covering the site—the most imperious disdain for economic height since J. P. Morgan's five-story headquarters at the corner of Wall and Broad Streets.

[1] Lever House profligately spent valuable square footage on open space, unthinkable today. [2] Lever House presented a leafy, suburban idyll in the city. [3] The window-washing platform that runs on steel tracks was widely imitated.

Seagram Building

375 PARK AVENUE » LUDWIG MIES VAN DER ROHE WITH PHILIP JOHNSON, DESIGN ARCHITECTS;

KAHN & JACOBS, ASSOCIATE ARCHITECTS, 1958

LTHOUGH GORDON Bunshaft designed the first all-glass curtain-wall building six years earlier just catercorner across Park Avenue, the Seagram Building remains the iconic glass box. Here was the *magister* delivering a seminar on his architecture of pure volume, structure, transparency, and reflection, and his sorcerer's apprentice Philip Johnson, completing the vision right down to the doorknobs. It was the most expensive building of its day, costing $36 million in addition to the $5-million land acquisition, and was the first building in the world with floor-to-ceiling glass walls.

The 38-story, 516-foot bronze-and-topaz-tinted glass slab is an expression of Mies van der Rohe's near-mystic faith in structure as the foundation of architecture. "Structure is spiritual," said Mies, who was even more gnomic than Le Corbusier. The Seagram's plan is based on a modular unit of four feet, seven and a half inches, followed throughout with a tolerance of only one-sixteenth of an inch, so that you always know where you are within a perfect, Cartesian grid. The structural columns are set 27 feet, nine inches apart in both directions, to form a classical ratio of five bays wide by three bays deep. In turn, the bays are divided by extruded bronze-covered I-beam mullions that run the entire length of the façade. The gridding of the pink Vermont granite plaza that runs under the plate-glass lobby walls to form the lobby floor also reflects the modular design.

Mies, more or less, worked on the same formalist problems his entire career—"One does not invent a new architecture every Monday morning," he said—balancing minimalist structure with pure volume and negative space. Set back 100 feet on a 200-foot-wide by 300-foot-deep block front of Park Avenue, the massless volume of the Seagram plays off magnificently against the plaza's negative space, achieving a unity in opposites. "The serene effect of pure space itself . . . has once again been recaptured," the critic Lewis

Mumford noted of the Seagram. In the monumental yet lighter-than-air lobby, interior and exterior space are perceived as continuous. Volume becomes contained space, visually balanced with mass and regulated by structure.

At a stroke, Mies replaced the setback skyscraper with a new paradigm: the glass tower in a plaza. The model was almost universally adopted after changes in the 1961 Zoning Code allowed developers extra height as a tradeoff for providing public amenities such as plazas and improved subway stops. Though visually inventive, the setback style, itself a response to 1916 Zoning Code changes, suddenly seemed as quaint and outmoded as a Flash Gordon film set in the face of Mies's austere aesthetic formulation. To achieve the perfect proportions of building and plaza in relation to the street, Mies assembled a mock-up of Park Avenue on a high table, so that he could sit and view it at eye level.

The Seagram is so powerful because its modernism is deeply rooted in the classical model. The bronze-clad *pilotis* lift the building above the ceremonial space of the plaza to establish it as an exercise in pure geometry. The bronze mullions of the façade are a brilliantly syncretic detail, referring at once to the structural properties of the Ionic pillar and the steel I beam that is the foundation of modern architecture. Like the classical Greek pillar, the miniature I beams enliven the façade with a play of light and shadow as a decorative device. Mies clearly meant the curtain wall to be perceived for what it is, a curtain or wrapping for the building: the mullions terminate just inches from the ground to show they are not structural.

Although the building presents itself as the ultimate manifestation of a machine-made, modular aesthetic, the design abounds in contradictions: in fact, it is the ultimate handmade

1

[1] The gridding of the pink Vermont granite plaza that runs under the plate-glass lobby walls. and the structural columns.
reflect the modular design.

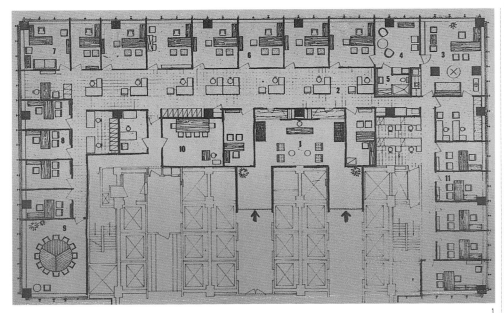

art object, going back to an earlier tradition of artisanship rather than factory production. Among its deviations from mass production, the mullions were custom-made specifically for the Seagram because Mies liked their crisp detailing. Even the screws that hold in the fixed glass-plate windows are made of brass. Because brass weathers, the building has to be hand-polished with a water-and-lemon spray annually to keep it from turning the color of the Statue of Liberty.

The lobby and ground-floor restaurants by Philip Johnson remain one of the city's gorgeous displays of high modernism. The range of inventiveness within a minimalist aesthetic is astonishing: the textile-like, cartridge-belt stainless steel and brass lining of the elevator cabs, the gold-anodized aluminum chain curtains in the Pool Room restaurant that sway gently in air currents from the vents, and the side canopies that are as nakedly structural as a dinosaur skeleton.

But the Seagram is not as structurally honest as its façade might indicate. The floor plates provide the only visual horizontal line, giving no indication of how the building is wind-braced (the braces are actually disguised in the elevator core, and in concrete bracing in the rear). The façade also does not tell you that much of the floor space is hidden in a T-shaped bustle behind the building. Some other details are curious: the 24-foot illuminated travertine lobby is a powerful corporate image, but the windowless conference rooms on the fourth floor are only nine feet tall.

The Seagram was a built at a time when American corporations were lining up their headquarters like iconic chess pieces on the playing board of Park Avenue: the new, improved Lever House; the globe-girdling colossus of the Pan Am; and the ever-young, aluminum-faced Pepsi Building (Gordon Bunshaft, 1960). The critic William Jordy noted that the bronze Seagram was "the first metal-and-glass skyscraper consciously designed to age as masonry buildings age—as appropriate for Seagram's whisky as sheen for Lever's soap." (As a footnote, Charles Luckman, the executive who commissioned Lever House and then returned to practice as an architect, designed a competing model for the Seagram with an oversized logo above the door that looked exactly like a gift-wrapped bottle of Scotch.)

[1] The tenth-floor plan.   [2] The Seagram is an archetype of modular design.

Time & Life Building

1271 SIXTH AVENUE » HARRISON & ABRAMOVITZ, 1959

WALLACE K. HARRISON'S Time & Life Building gets short shrift in architectural accounts of New York, yet its banded limestone-and-glass façade was one of the most-imitated prototypes for midtown skyscrapers. Harrison saw his design as a pragmatic solution to the client's demands: as much floor space as possible to accommodate the magazine's expanding staff, and a relation to the older buildings of Rockefeller Center across the avenue. The result is a crisp corporate update, the architectural equivalent of the striped shirts, sack suits, and rep ties that Harrison favored.

The postwar aesthetic was the pure expression of structure. Harrison started from the outside in, placing the steel supporting columns outside the floor area to create a free span of 32,500 square feet from exterior wall to the core on each floor. The columns, set 28 feet apart, are sheathed in limestone on the exterior to complement Raymond Hood's design for Rockefeller Center, which Harrison also worked on. The Time & Life's grid of dark metal-framed, smoked-glass windows with opaque mesh spandrels set behind the glass and protruding aluminum mullions expresses the building's basic modular layout. The building terminates with the Internationalist disdain for cornices, as if the height was determined solely by economic and structural concerns, rather than anything so superfluous as "style."

The proportion of the lightweight piers in the glassy face is a transition toward abandoning stone façades entirely. In the postwar economy, rising construction costs and a dearth of skilled stoneworkers led architects to embrace the glass box, as seen in the metastasis of inferior knock-offs. The Time & Life parti was copied in a number of buildings on Avenue of the Americas in the West 50s, including Skidmore, Owings & Merrill's Equitable Life Building (1961), Emery Roth's Sperry-Rand (1962) and ABC Buildings (1965), William B. Tabler's Hilton Hotel (1963), and Shreve, Lamb & Harmon's J. C. Penney Building (1965). The copycat quality of the buildings actually adds a pleasing architectural unity to the area, with its broad, plaza-like sidewalks and retroceding glass boxes.

The Time & Life Building was constructed before the 1961 revision of the zoning code that allowed builders extra height in exchange for developing public plazas, so the corporation had to buy the Roxy Theater to the west in order to acquire its air rights. With the air rights, the 48-story tower occupied only one quarter of its lot, as mandated by the old code.

The plaza and lobby are a bright spot of 1960s-style optimism. The wavy-gravy terrazzo pattern employed by Harrison at the UN sweeps from the azure-colored fountain through the plate glass doors into the lobby. Alar, cantilevered aluminum canopies project over the entrances like V-for-victory signs. Architects of the era may have felt a bit guilty about foisting the abstract art on an uneducated public. A Mondrianesque mural by Fritz Glarner is accompanied by an explanatory note: "The artist considers the theme of this abstract mural to be the rhythm and movement of the city."

[1] Decorative panels alternated with sweeping city views at the Hemisphere Club, a bar and lounge (now closed) in the Time & Life.   [2] The bar at the Hemisphere Club, shown here in 1960.

Union Carbide Building

(now Chase Manhattan Bank)　　　270 PARK AVENUE　»　SKIDMORE, OWINGS & MERRILL, 1960

O FTEN GLOSSED over as a Skidmore, Owings & Merrill clone of the Seagram Building, the Union Carbide is a bold commitment to Internationalism as a sculptural aesthetic. Within the Miesian architectural framework of pure structuralism, SOM's principal partner Gordon Bunshaft was interested in pursuing the same esoteric questions that minimalist sculptors such as Tony Smith, David Smith, Donald Judd, and Isamu Noguchi were engaging with: What is the nature of the relationship between viewer and object; What are the effects of scale; What constitutes a material's surface; and What is the interplay between two-dimensional and three-dimensional forms?

The 25-foot-high glass-walled lobby, designed by Natalie de Blois, one of the few women in the man's world of Internationalism, and the interior designer Jack G. Dunbar, neatly articulates the building's structure with color. The weightless, wraparound skin of the 41-story tower's lobby is clear glass, the supporting columns are black matte finish, the plaza and lobby floor are gray granite, the soffits are white, the trim is stainless steel, and the walls of the elevator core are a startling red under a luminous white plastic ceiling.

Like the minimalists, Bunshaft was beginning to look at his buildings simply as objects in the world. His materials become increasingly specific, and are used for their objective qualities. As Donald Judd said of sculpture in the same period: "Most of the work involves new materials, either recent inventions or things not used before in art. . . . Materials vary greatly and are simply materials—Formica, aluminum, cold-rolled steel, Plexiglas, red and common brass, and so forth. They are specific. If they are used directly, they are more specific. Also, they are usually aggressive. There is an objectivity to the obdurate identity of a material."

The red elevator core is aggressive in Judd's sense, because it confronts us with the issue of surface. As the critic Michael Fried points out in *Art and Objecthood*, "the color of a given sculpture, whether applied or in the natural state of the material, is identical with its surface; and inasmuch as all objects have surface, awareness of the sculpture's surface implies its objecthood." Particularly at night, when the red core glows like a rocket flame under the black bulk of the building, we are confronted with the objecthood of this building.

The building is based on a five-foot module with 20-foot-wide by 40-foot-deep bays, but the big red core is what turns an ordinary structure into a sculptural object. We are first challenged by the question of its scale: How big is it, and how big are we in relation to it? Tony Smith was once questioned about his six-foot cube *Die* (1962), "Why didn't you make it larger so that it would loom over the observer?" "I was not making a monument," Smith said. "Then why didn't you make it smaller so that the observer could see over the top?" "I was not making an object," Smith said. Because the Union Carbide disorients us as to its scale, we are invited to perceive the building for its sculptural, rather than just architectural, qualities.

The Union Carbide is flawed architecturally: its awkwardly proportioned plaza is a dead zone, rather than a true public space, and the protruding stainless steel mullions are coarsely derivative of the hand-tooled perfection of the Seagram façade. But it is too easy to overlook that Gordon Bunshaft was reconstruing architecture as minimalist sculpture, as radical a departure as modern architecture was from the Renaissance architecture of mass and form, light and shadow.

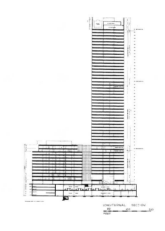

[1] The lobby masterfully uses minimalist materials to define its structure.　[2] The tower is supported on steel pilings above the Park Avenue subway lines.　[3] The elevators are to the rear, right, to maximize the tower's open floor space.

Chase Manhattan Plaza

LIBERTY AND NASSAU STREETS » SKIDMORE, OWINGS & MERRILL, 1961

F OR BETTER and worse, it was
Rockefeller money that revitalized
New York in the 1960s, when corporations were writing off American cities
at fire-sale prices. Chase Manhattan Plaza, the
sleek $121-million headquarters of David
Rockefeller's bank, was the start of a new wave
of office construction in the lagging financial
district. Chase was also a prime mover in financ-
ing such megaprojects as Lincoln Center, the
World Trade Center, South Street Seaport, and
Madison Square Garden.

Although flawed architecturally, Chase
Manhattan Plaza is significant because it represents the Internationalists' attitude toward the
old city infrastructure: stamp on it like Godzilla
and build over it. The sheer, 60-story, 813-foot-
tall aluminum-and-glass-sheathed tower contains 1.8 million square feet. The building's two-
and-a-half-acre plot realigned the old street patterns by "demapping" (literally, removing a
street from the city plan) a block of Cedar Street
to form a superblock, bordered by Pine, Liberty,
William, and Nassau Streets. Chase was the first
tower in a plaza built downtown under the new
Zoning Code of 1961 and led the way for other
plazas including Marine Midland, Liberty Plaza,
the World Trade Center, and the World
Financial Center.

Individual parts of this building are better
than the sum. Its big-shouldered parti is monotonous, and seems to muscle aside the surrounding delicate stone towers of the 1930s. It is top

heavy, and Bunshaft later said he was dissatisfied
with the undernourished columns and the
"emphasis on vertical ribbons." But the shining,
anodized-aluminum skin stood out among the
dark towers of Wall Street like a newly minted
coin. Bunshaft seemed to be reaching back to
the glittering treasure metaphors of the Chrysler
and Cass Gilbert's gold-pyramided New York
Life Insurance Company Building (1928) for references. Among the best details are the aggressively minimalist interior walls of the below-
grade plaza, where surfaces are defined by single
colors. The views from the top-floor executive
lounge are Zeus-like, on eye-level with the green
bronze pyramidal top of 40 Wall.

Chase is a transition from the building as
an object to which you apply sculpture to the
building itself as a sculptural object. As if apolo-
getic for not giving the public enough with the
architecture, Rockefeller allotted a kingly
$500,000 for the plaza's art budget. Bunshaft, a
connoisseur of modern art, approached Isamu
Noguchi, who was well represented in
Bunshaft's private collection, to design the
Sunken Garden (1964). The garden, set 16 feet
below grade, consists of seven basalt stones from
the bed of the Uji River in Kyoto that seem to
float on concentric patterns of paving. The garden also functions like a Roman oculus, letting
daylight into the banking floor below. Jean
Dubuffet's papery-looking, 42-foot-high *Group
of Four Trees* was added in 1972. Although
appealing in their own right, neither sculpture
relates particularly well to the slab, and Bunshaft
would find a more successful aesthetic resolution
with his masterful Marine Midland Bank plaza.

[1] Dubuffet's GROUP OF FOUR TREES adorns Chase Plaza.   [2] The Chase, right, epitomized the postwar push for sheer
floor space in buildings.   [3] A waving flag indicates the Chase has topped out in September, 1959.   [4] Chase construction workers gather for a group photo in 1959.

Pan Am Building

(now Met Life Building)

200 PARK AVENUE » WALTER GROPIUS, PIETRO BELLUSCHI, AND RICHARD ROTH OF EMERY ROTH & SONS, 1963

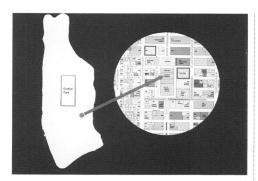

THE YEAR 1963 was traumatic for city lovers. First, McKim, Mead & White's supernal Pennsylvania Station (1910) was dismantled stone by stone and hauled off to a dump in New Jersey, only to be replaced by the meretricious, mean-spirited Madison Square Garden. Second, a foreboding giant blotted out the sky over Park Avenue. This giant—the Pan Am Building—and the imminent destruction of the jewel in the city's diadem, Grand Central Terminal, finally woke up citizens to the fact that they might be losing something valuable in exchange for all the new construction. The New York City Landmarks Preservation Commission was formed two years later.

The 55-story, 808-foot-tall Pan Am, built at a cost of $100 million and clad in precast concrete panels, is vilified more for where it is than what it is. Not only did the Pan Am wander off the grid, but it had the effrontery to turn its broad side uptown, violating Manhattan's traditional north-south alignment. The ultimate responsibility for siting the broad slab across one of the city's most pleasant and open boulevards was Walter Gropius's. Internationalist monuments apparently were not meant to be enjoyed from the sidewalk: Gropius referred to Europe's great cities as "stony deserts" and prophesied that, "Seen from the skies, the leafy house-tops of the cities of the future will look like endless chains of hanging gardens." Pietro Belluschi defended the design from an urbanist point of view: "I'd like to put in a good word for urban congestion," he said. "It's an excitement you can only find in New York City."

What New Yorkers were left with was a coarse rip-off of Gio Ponti and Luigi Nervi's trimly elegant Pirelli Building (Milan, 1959), which itself had historical roots in Florence's Palazzo Vecchio of 1314. From the east and west, the elongated octagon of the Pan Am with its narrow ends works quite well as a campanile. The façade of the 47-story tower above an eight-story platform that matches the cornice of Grand Central Terminal is broken into three sections by recessing the curtain wall behind the columns, throwing deep shadows. Unfortunately, concrete does not age well—even the Solomon R. Guggenheim Museum looks more like a potsherd than a new building—so that the Pan Am, one of New York's monuments, resembles nothing more than a gritty sidewalk. In addition, the building emits a grating, high-frequency sound that mimics a bird in distress, to keep away pigeons. When it opened in April 1963, the 2.4-million-square-foot building was the largest, rather than the tallest, office building in the world, and was an instant success: 93 percent of the space was already leased.

The Pan Am represents not only the postwar disdain for history and emphasis on sheer burgeoning floor space, but continues the modernist love affair with transportation. The banks of whooshing escalators that connect the Pan Am with the Beaux-Arts elegance of Grand Central's concourse are one of its most successful elements. Fourteen escalators connect the through-block Pan Am concourse with 61 passenger elevators at the second floor lobby level, in a dream of efficiency in motion. (Normally below grade, the elevator pits are on the first floor, because the tracks of the Metro North Railroad run under the Pan Am.) Like the over-the-top transportation fantasies in the Chanin and Empire State buildings, the Pan Am's roof was used as a helicopter landing pad until a fatal accident in 1977. Frank Lloyd Wright anticipated the use of helipads on tall buildings with his visionary Mile High Illinois project of 1956.

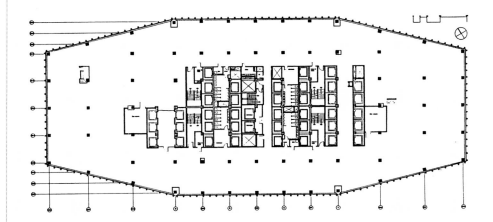

[1] A map emphasizing the building's ideal midtown location was included in a promotional packet for prospective tenants.

[2] A typical floor plan of the office space, this one on the 18th Floor.

CBS Building

51 WEST 52ND STREET » EERO SAARINEN, 1965

ERO SAARINEN said he wanted to make the "simplest skyscraper in New York" with his sheer, 38-story, 490-foot-tall headquarters for CBS. This is the only skyscraper designed by Saarinen, who died in 1961, without seeing his building completed.

The tower is elegantly conceived and structurally innovative. Rib-like salient columns support the weight of the building, lashed together by the floor plates and anchored by the reinforced concrete elevator core. It was the first building in New York to use pillars made of reinforced concrete rather than a steel frame. Because the 35-foot-deep floor plates on the 135-by-160-foot site have no internal columns, the building contains an ample 800,000 square feet of office space. This is a tower without tricks: there are no hidden bustles like those of the Seagram or the Citicorp to make up floor space. Saarinen fulfilled his Sullivanesque joy in creating a "building that would stand firmly on the ground and grow straight up."

Five-foot-wide triangular columns clad in black granite project from a surface of smoked glass and black granite spandrels, which accounts for the tower's Gothic nickname, Black Rock. The façade functions like a minimalist sculpture: seen obliquely, the piers seem to form a solid wall but appear open and glassy when viewed directly. There is a tremendous visual energy as the observer walks around the building, and the piers ripple open and closed like accordion pleats.

Few other buildings succeed so directly in making the viewer aware of the building as both a container of space and as a volume of space. The windows of gray-tinted vision glass play tantalizingly with the relationship of surface and interior space: from some angles the interior lights can be seen, and from other viewpoints the windows reflect only sky. The black skin was enormously important in Gordon Bunshaft's thinking for another minimalist masterpiece, his Marine Midland Bank.

Saarinen wanted the sculptural qualities of his building to be appreciated, so he set it apart

in its own plaza, which has been criticized for its lack of urban contextualism. But Saarinen felt he was being considerate of the streetscape: "We tried to place the building on the site so that we could have a plaza and still not destroy the street line," he said. "A plaza is a very necessary thing in a city. It lets people sit in the sun and look at the sky. . . . These arrangements should be orderly and beautiful so the streets do not look like torn things and the towers like isolated teeth sticking up from a gaping mouth." Yet Saarinen's sunless, seatless, and sunken plaza would appear to be the antithesis of what he had in mind. No one uses it, except to nip through the midblock, and it is too shallow even to get a good look at the building. The plaza can be thought of as a forbidding moat around a castle, in keeping with the Gothic theme.

In a number of ways, the CBS is the last great Gothic tower in Manhattan. Because it is supported by masonry rather than a steel cage, its antecedants date to John Wellborn Root and Daniel Burnham's Monadnock Building (1884–1991), and it is a refinement of Raymond Hood's dark American Radiator Building. Although the projecting piers terminate at the flat roofline, they visually appear to form crenellations, a vestigial trace of Gothicism.

[1] Los Angeles's CBS Building (c. 1950) reflects the strong Bauhaus influence on West Coast architecture, an interesting contrast to the Black Rock of 1960s Manhattan.   [2] Early Byrds: members of the California-based rock group the Byrds flock at the base of Black Rock after signing with CBS Records.

Silver Towers

(originally University Plaza)

100 AND 110 BLEECKER STREET, AND 505 LAGUARDIA PLACE »

I. M. PEI, 1966

BUILT AS housing for New York University faculty and graduate students, I. M. Pei's Silver Towers has all the earmarks of a high-modernist superblock: demapped streets, slabs without relation to surrounding buildings, ample underground parking, and unused greenswards. Though usually mentioned only in connection with its centerpiece Picasso sculpture, Silver Towers is a fine composition that creates a modernist dialogue between openness and enclosure.

The sheer, 30-story, reinforced concrete and glass towers are an elegant synthesis of many strains of modernist design, and at the same time express Pei's minimalist sculptural sensibility. A "slightly skeptical acolyte" of Walter Gropius, in the words of his biographer Michael Cannell, Pei clearly expresses the structure of Silver Towers, but improves on Gropius's unlovely precast concrete façade for the Pan Am Building. The warm, buff-colored concrete façades of the three Silver Towers are organized into four by eight structural bays of deeply recessed plate-glass windows. The wedge-shaped

piers and sloping windowsills soften what would otherwise be a cold, office-building-like grid.

The articulated concrete frame with deep-set windows gives the impression of a sheltering, lithic building, yet at the same time forms an open cage of space. The façades are sculptural because the bays vary from open glass panels to completely recessed stone frames. The transitional points on the façades between a regular grid and sharp zigzags change, depending upon which angle they are viewed from, so that the buildings always have a kinetic sense of energy. Backgrounded against the low-set, landmarked neighborhood of SoHo, few skyscraper complexes have so much open sky around them, and the flow of space is almost palpable. The buildings are set on a pinwheel plan, and seem to swim forward in space.

Pei wanted to provide a sense of home comfort: the glassed-in, Miesian lobby is counterbalanced with a traditional wall of buff brick to provide a human scale. Like Le Corbusier's cast concrete collective housing unit, Unité d'Habitation (1947–53) in Marseilles, the build-

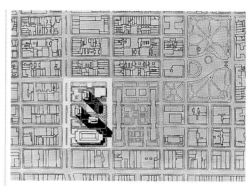

2

ing interacts naturally with environment: the deeply overhanging soffits function like a *brise-soleil*, and the windows slide open for natural air circulation. "There were no teachers to teach us the new architecture," Pei recalls of his early education in Shanghai before he attended the Massachusetts Institute of Technology, "so we turned to Corbu's books, and these were responsible for half our education." Le Corbusier's influence can be seen even in Pei's choice of round, horn-rim eyewear.

Pei also used the deep window sockets to provide a sense of privacy and shelter, the way Frank Lloyd Wright did. "I know you," Frank Lloyd Wright said upon meeting Pei. "You belong to Zeckendorf." It took the slightly built, self-assured Pei a number of years to emerge from the shadow of his reputation as the in-house architect for the megadeveloper William Zeckendorf.

Bust of Sylvette, the 36-foot-tall, 60-ton, concrete interpretation by the Swedish sculptor Carl Nesjar of the much smaller Picasso bronze, sits in the center of the plaza. The porous perimeter of the towers provides a nice balance between openness and enclosure.

1

[1] The wedge-shaped piers and sloping windowsills soften what would otherwise be a cold, office-building-like grid.

[2] The site plan shows the three-block setting.

Marine Midland Bank Building

(now 140 Broadway)

GORDON BUNSHAFT, 1967

things, we are now offered the illusion of modalities: namely, that matter is incorporeal, weightless, and exists only optically like a mirage."

The Marine Midland is transcendent architecture because it presents an office building frankly, as a container of commercial space (we can see through its reflective and transparent skin), but at the same time, the containment of space becomes the image of the building itself in the form of flat rhomboidal planes. The commercial and aesthetic functions of the building are one. Arthur Drexler, director of the Museum of Modern Art's architecture and design department wrote about Marine Midland: "The 'function' of the building is recognized as analogous to that of a package; what is offered is a commodity: portions of space."

Minimalism was the final expression of the unified aesthetic of modernism. "The era of the 1960s, as epitomized by Minimal art, saw the future optimistically," wrote the critic Frances Colpitt. "It evidenced an unmatchable enthusiasm for progressive invention and a passionate commitment to intellectual inquiry. It was, *then*, a world without fragmentation, a world of seamless unity." The Marine Midland is one of the last, best expressions of modernist unity. After architecture had been reduced to such a purely visual form, the question became where to go from there. In retrospect, the return to symbolism, fragmentation, and discontinuity of postmodernism seem inevitable.

GORDON BUNSHAFT'S designs have been widely imitated for all the wrong reasons. Like his seminal Lever House, his Marine Midland Bank Building, sheathed in flush black glass, was appreciated more for its skin than its parti. After Marine Midland, everybody raced to build in black and flush glass, but few understood Bunshaft's underlying minimalist sculptural aesthetic.

Marine Midland was not the first flush glass curtain-wall building; Pietro Belluschi had done it with his extraordinarily far-sighted Equitable Life Assurance Building (1944–47) in Portland, Oregon. Bunshaft further explored minimalist questions of the relation of surface to volume, and opticality versus objecthood. The entire composition of the white travertine plaza, Isamu Noguchi's vermilion sculpture *Cube* (1973), and the trapezoidal, 51-story black tower form brilliant variations on the relationship of two-dimensional and three-dimensional space.

Bunshaft took his leitmotif from the irregular site itself, bordered by Cedar, Liberty, and Nassau Streets and Broadway. Seen from the air, the way an architect would look at it on a blue-print, the block forms a two-dimensional rhomboid. The building's footprint is trapezoidal, wider on the Nassau Street front with four bays tapering to three bays on Broadway. The resulting acute and oblique angles make the façades appear to be purely two-dimensional surfaces. Because the walls of bronzed glass and black matte anodized aluminum are so flat and without scale, the parallax effect of their height becomes more apparent, and they in turn recreate the plaza's irregular rhomboidal angle.

Noguchi's 28-foot-tall elongated cube in the plaza is a densely layered synthesis of the architectural themes. The rhombohedron seems to be pulled out of two-dimensional space, a transitional object between the flat canvas of the plaza and the three-dimensional tower. Noguchi also plays with the idea of surface and space: the cube has a hole drilled through it, so that it is seen simultaneously as surface and as container of space. "To render substance entirely optical, and form, whether pictorial, sculptural, or architectural, as an integral part of ambient space—this brings anti-illusionism full circle," wrote art critic Clement Greenberg. "Instead of the illusion of

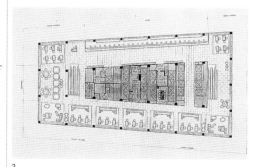

General Motors Building

767 FIFTH AVENUE » EDWARD DURELL STONE; EMERY ROTH & SONS, ASSOCIATE ARCHITECTS, 1968

AFTER BEING summarily drummed out of the Internationalist ranks for his kitschy One Columbus Circle (1958, now slated for the wrecking ball possibly to make way for nothing more than another redundant plaza), Edward Durell Stone designed his first skyscraper, the New York headquarters and showroom for General Motors. The 50-story tower with stubby wings is an interesting, albeit failed attempt to transcend Internationalism's "glass-boxitis," as Philip Johnson called it.

Stone was a lone voice in the wilderness when he defied the high-modernist orthodoxy of the late 1960s. "I am critical of the steel and glass monolithic structures, inspired by Mies," he said, "particularly the type one finds along Park Avenue now, because I believe architecture should be more permanent in character." Stone's method of making the GM more "permanent" was to return to the skyscraper's masonry origins in the Chicago School. The GM Building's three-sided, alternating bays of white marble and black glass recall the oriels of Chicago's Manhattan Building (William Le Baron Jenney, 1891), one

of the last great stone-supported tall buildings, and Daniel Burnham's Flatiron Building. Perhaps to lend an air of modernity, Stone called his glass bays "vision panels," and pointed out their energy efficiency. Because the bays provided views up and down the avenue, Stone said that they "give the occupant of each office a welcome sense of individuality." Oddly, the paper-white slab resembles nothing so much as that icon of 1960s impersonality, the IBM punch card.

Stone's problem was that he single-handedly tried to find a way out of the glass box that modernism built itself into, without post-modernism's theoretical apparatus of discontinuity and pastiche. The GM is a failed offshoot because Stone tried to incorporate historicism into modernism's unyielding mold, rather than to explore and celebrate the discontinuities, as later architects did. Stone wandered into increasingly idiosyncratic, filigreed masonry designs, and his career remains in critical neglect.

Emery Roth & Sons, the associate architects on the GM Building, did more to change the face of Manhattan than any single builder. Between 1950 and 1970, the firm built a whopping 30 million square feet of office space, or half the total created in that period. They cared little for the building's external wrapper. What they delivered was the belly of the beast: maximum open-plan floor space, high-speed elevators, and advanced climate control systems. Roth "econo-boxes" completely changed the character of Third Avenue in midtown after the El was ripped out in 1955.

The GM's moribund sunken plaza, deserted even in the best of weather, is often cited as an example of poor urban planning. "To achieve the most bulk possible under the new law, it will have an open plaza facing an existing plaza," the critic Ada Louise Huxtable wrote about the siting across the avenue from Grand Army Plaza's urbane fountain and statue of General Sherman. "Ever hear of a redundant plaza? This is it."

[1] Since the 1960s, the GM showroom has featured their latest model cars. [2] The slim-lined GM Building was an early attempt to break out of the glass box.

One Astor Plaza

1515 BROADWAY » DER SCUTT OF KAHN & JACOBS, 1972

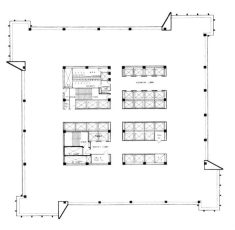

ONE ASTOR PLAZA'S tower, a sharply angled limestone crown by Der Scutt, the lead architect for the project for Kahn & Jacobs, is a significant precursor of postmodernism's movement away from structural expression and toward symbolism for its own sake. By placing a non-functional crown—and a stone one at that—atop a glass building, Der Scutt was beginning to undermine basic Internationalist assumptions such as the ban on applied symbolism. The spiky crown was even more affronting in 1972 when it featured the giant orange logo of the W. T. Grant five-and-dime chain.

The 54-story building seems to be assembled from pieces of other buildings; Der Scutt was one of the first architects to employ this kind of pastiche. Flaring limestone pylons stick out from the sides of the tower, sheathed in black glass superimposed with sectional aluminum mullions. Oddly projecting glass bays at the corners anticipate Der Scutt's experiments with the glass curtain wall in such later buildings as

Trump Tower. With a budding postmodernist's sense for sleight of hand, the blank mass of the Astor Plaza movie theater on West 44th Street is revealed from another angle as a thin façade, because its wall projects beyond the cornice.

Built on the site of the old Astor Hotel and its celebrated bar, Astor Plaza epitomizes the antiurban sentiment of planners in the late 1960s. Rather than a congested, vital urban arena, Times Square, with some justification, was seen as a seedy breeding ground of pornography and crime. The solution was to eradicate street life, and turn the neighborhood into a parched and untraversable desert like Oscar Niemeyer's designs for the main state institutions in Brasilia, Brazil. Astor Plaza was the first building to exploit an easement of the 1961 Zoning Code that allowed developers to put up taller and bulkier than usual buildings as an incentive to build new legitimate theaters in the ailing Theater District.

The 327-foot by 201-foot plot is simply huge, absorbing the entire half-block bordered

by the pedestrian corridor of Shubert Alley, except for a token fringe of minuscule plazas. The office tower, containing 1.4 million square feet, is set back 135 feet from the Broadway front. The blind, five-story concrete wall of the Astor Plaza movie theater is as overtly hostile to the street as the Marriott Marquis next door: together, the buildings resemble a phalanx of stone policemen making sure that nobody actually lingers on the street.

The building also contains the lavish 1,621-seat Minskoff Theater, which is large enough to handle Broadway musicals and is entered through a covered plaza in the building's center. The underground Astor Plaza movie theater is one of the great, latter-day movie palaces with 1,500 seats and 1960s-style leopard-skin carpeting. The dual function of office building and entertainment complex (MTV has studios here) is an extension of the design for the Deco-era Paramount Building just down the street, and shows that what keeps a building vital is that it meets a city's many needs.

[1] The Minskoff Theater creates a glittering array of lights at night. [2] The pinwheel motif is carried though in a typical tower floor. [3] The ground floor reflects multiuse for theaters and rental office space.

XYZ Buildings

Exxon Building 1251 AVENUE OF THE AMERICAS » HARRISON, ABRAMOVITZ & HARRIS, 1971

McGraw-Hill Building 1221 AVENUE OF THE AMERICAS, 1973

Celanese Building 1211 AVENUE OF THE AMERICAS, 1974

1

FEW HAVE kind words for this super complex of three nearly identical towers built as an extension of Rockefeller Center on the west side of Sixth Avenue. Even Wallace Harrison's biographer, Victoria Newhouse, calls them "monotonous," "tedious," "overbearing," and "arid"—all in one paragraph. Yet they form the background texture of one of city's most viable and densely utilized areas, just south of Central Park. How can both assessments be true?

The buildings are most criticized for their prosaic presentation of the tall office building as shoe boxes for commercial space; in fact, the slabs were considered so interchangeable that they were called "the XYZ plan." Harrison originally wanted to enliven their profiles by setting

the slabs in a voguish pinwheel formation, but this would have probably made them more distracting rather than more interesting. Harrison's original scheme had more in common with the original Rockefeller Center across the avenue: the three slabs framing a large, landscaped, sunken plaza, with the McGraw-Hill Building oriented north-south along a private street. In shaky block lettering, Harrison wrote across a copy of this plan, "My scheme for the west side turned down by"—two names are then scratched out, but the second is plainly legible, "Mike Harris," the associate architect. By the time the Celanese Building was completed in 1974, Harrison was nearly 80, and was becoming a seigniorial background figure in the firm; new clients asked for Max Abramowitz.

The very anonymity of the XYZ buildings works to their advantage in forming a kind of abstract, gridded background that thrusts the avenue into the foreground. These are surely among the most reticent towers ever built. The McGraw-Hill and Exxon (originally Standard Oil) Buildings sit back 117 feet from the avenue to create plazas with extra-wide sidewalks. From certain angles up and down the avenue, the towers seem to disappear entirely, freeing up the sky around them. This receding visual quality is heightened by the towers' lack of scale. Supernumerary piers, twice as many as are structurally necessary, splinter the façades into thin vertical strips. Continuous bands of opaque glass spandrels and bronzed-glass windows provide no indication of floor levels.

In plan and in their façade treatments, the XYZ towers are essentially knockoffs of Harrison's earlier and better Time & Life Building, down to their alar cantilevered canopies, but lack the original's clarity of structural expression. The 54-story, 784-foot-high, 2.1 million-square-foot Exxon Building (1967–71) was the first of the three to be built. The structural exoskeleton, which holds the building up without internal columns, is clad in limestone as a contextual tribute to the older Rockefeller Center buildings across the avenue. The 51-story, 645-foot-tall, 1.8-million-square-foot McGraw-Hill Building, clad in plummy red granite, was completed in 1973. The 45-story, 1.6-million-square-foot Celanese Building varied only slightly from the others in that it had a smaller, L-shaped plaza, and the glass and limestone façade formed a nearly flush curtain.

The XYZ plan is the closest approximation of what Le Corbusier's proposed City of Towers would look like in the context of Manhattan, or what a city might be like if it were all designed by one person. In fact, the

[1] The site for the new McGraw-Hill Building was a motley assortment of bars and small shops.

towers do not eliminate the traditional Rue Corridor, but create a new one. "Typical Plan is empty as possible: a floor, a core, a perimeter, and a minimum of columns," Rem Koolhaas writes in his *S,M,L,XL*. "It's unsung designers—Bunshaft, Harrison and Abramovitz, Emery Roth—represent vanishing acts so successful that they are now completely forgotten."

The XYZ buildings have as much impact for what is not there as for what is there. The open space between the square-topped towers makes the observer aware of the vast volume of space contained behind their subdued, pinstriped exteriors. The forthright geometrical silhouettes cut the sky into vibrant patterns. There is a certain satisfying corporate symbolism at work here: bluff, no-nonsense, but restrained behind a business-like front.

Unfortunately, almost everybody, including Nelson and John D. Rockefeller Jr., hated the buildings. "Nelson criticized the Sixth Avenue buildings and said John didn't like them either," Harrison recalled. "There was a complete change of attitude. Nelson said he wouldn't give me any more work.... I was broken-hearted about it. What the hell, I had done the very best I knew how."

Critics differ on whether the plazas work or not, but they are a lively part of the urban fabric, and are well used in good weather. "Perhaps the key to success here is that whatever these buildings are doing to the public space of the city they are doing it together," wrote the critic Gerald Allen when they opened. The vest-pocket parks, frequently an afterthought, are quite intimate and pleasant. The park in back of the McGraw-Hill Building features a walk-through waterfall that recalls Harrison's design for the Electric Utilities Exhibit at the 1939 World's Fair.

As Cesar Pelli remarked "Cities are made up of foreground and background buildings, yet no one, whether architect or client, wants to do a background building. Therefore, all our

2

buildings need to be both foreground and background." The XYZ buildings fail in the foreground because of their lack of style, but are overlooked as among the city's best background buildings.

The lower concourses, meant primarily for the 80,000 office workers on the east and west sides of Rockefeller Center, are unadvertised at street level and are remarkably well used. The social effects of turning street life into private property could be debated: these "streets" are patrolled by watchful private security forces. It could also be argued that turning the street life inward is part of a "malling" or "themeing" of American life, along the lines of James Rouse, who created the Faneuil Hall Marketplace (1976) in Boston, and Manhattan's South Street Seaport (1984).

[1] The Exxon Building, to the left of the empty lots, was the first of the three buildings to be completed.

[2] The waterfall outside Wallace K. Harrison's consolidated Edison's City of Light exhibition at the 1939 New York World's Fair resembles the park behind the McGraw-Hill Building.

W. R. Grace Building

1114 AVENUE OF THE AMERICAS (ALSO 41 WEST 42ND STREET) » GORDON BUNSHAFT, 1973

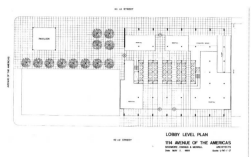

LOBBY LEVEL PLAN
1114 AVENUE OF THE AMERICAS
SKIDMORE, OWINGS & MERRILL   ARCHITECTS

1

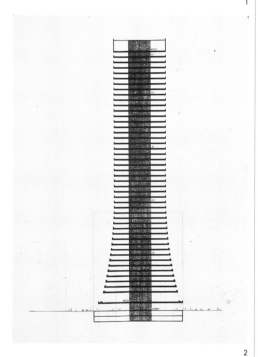

2

THIS IS Internationalism's last gasp; the brilliant minimalist opticality of Gordon Bunshaft's Marine Midland becomes a gimmicky optical illusion in the ski-shaped, 47-story, white-travertine and bronzed-glass W. R. Grace Building. Bunshaft seems to have explored Mies's reductionist aesthetic as far as it would go and in the end only found a structure devoid of symbolic value. The Grace Building literally seems to be stretching to find some new meaning that might be provided by postmodernism.

Bunshaft arrived at the building's shape by covering the setbacks required by the Zoning Code with a smooth, curved wall instead of angular steps. "We got the idea that instead of going up straight on the property line and then setting back . . . we would keep reducing the floors as we went up, on a curved line from the second floor," he told his biographer, Carol Hershelle Krinsky in 1988. "I don't think a building is very handsome with a big podium 86 feet high and then a tower set way back," he continued, somewhat defensively, considering that the headquarters for the giant chemical company stands on 42nd Street among some of the best examples of the setback style. "That is ugly and we still feel it is ugly. If we had a similar job today, we would probably do it somewhat like we did then." Bunshaft also designed the similarly sloped, 49-story, 725-foot-tall 9 West 57th Street, completed a year later as a real-estate venture.

The Grace Building's tapering façade, organized into seven rectangular, bronzed-glass window bays divided by travertine-covered piers, is always good for a double-take the first time someone sees it, but eventually passersby start to ignore it altogether—there is simply not enough going on here, beyond the fact that the illusion of concavity produced by towering vertical elements is exaggerated. Classical architects employed entasis, a rounded swelling in the center of their columns, to counteract this illusion, which is caused by the curvature of the human eyeball. The façade also makes use of the "phantom square" optical illusion, in which grayish squares seem to appear at the intersections of the white lines. The interior blinds are set in special tracks so that they do not hang vertically and spoil the sweeping effect.

Rather than reinterpreting and refining classicism as Mies did, Bunshaft is reduced to making visual puns. The building is classically organized—the piers are arranged like columns on a stylobate above a projecting second-floor travertine ledge that acts as a rain gutter—but the variations are symbolically empty. The sloping piers pierce the ledge to provide an open-glass ground floor. In better buildings, the effect is of weightlessness, of volumes floating on air, but here the curved legs are kitschy, like the cute slanted feet on a 1950s davenport.

The Grace Building is not a building for the ages, but its location on the border of Bryant Park and its idiosyncratic design solution make it one of the city's most visually prominent skyscrapers. The building was criticized mainly for breaking with the traditional wall of buildings that line the park. Bunshaft spoke resignedly about contextualism: "In New York City, if you built to conform with your neighbors in some cases before you were finished your neighbors would be demolished."

[1] Travertine paving extends to the curb on 42nd Street and in an open plaza, upper left.   [2] The Grace's broad lower floor plates taper up to the regular shaft.

1 and 2 World Trade Center

CHURCH TO WEST STREETS AND LIBERTY TO VESEY STREETS »

MINORU YAMASAKI AND EMERY ROTH & SONS, 1973 AND 1974

[1] A rendering of the original Twin Towers with the Woolworth Building in the foreground.

OUT OF A FLAWLESS blue sky at 8:46 in the morning on September 11, 2001 the unthinkable happened—a hijacked 767 airliner rammed into the 91st floor of the South Tower of the World Trade Center. Sixteen minutes later, a second jet hit the 81st floor of the North Tower and burst into flames. By 10:28 a.m. the towers had collapsed, and what were once the tallest buildings in the world became a smoldering ruin at the cost of 2,823 lives.

In their 28-year history, the Twin Towers had gone from being one of the more openly criticized features of the skyline to one of the most popular. The stunningly minimalist design, which at first seemed to upend the skyline because of its sheer scale, was designed by Minoru Yamasaki, an unlikely choice for lead architect of the megadevelopment. He was not one of the troika of Internationalist corporate architects: Gordon Bunshaft, Wallace K.

Harrison, and Edward Durell Stone (before his apostasy); he was best known for modestly scaled, sculptural buildings such as his 30-story Reynolds Building in Detroit (1958); and he was morbidly afraid of heights. The design he delivered was even more unusual: not a glass slab at all but twin towers, supported by external columns, that function as minimalist sculpture.

Like the Empire State Building, which it superseded by a calculated 100 feet, the World Trade Center was a marvel of logistics and engineering. Its sheer bulk was difficult to take in: two sheer, flat-topped, 110-story, 1,362- and 1,368-foot-tall towers, which together contain an unheard-of 10 million square feet of office space. Each floor took up an entire acre because of the column-free floor plates and the distribution of elevators.

The list of construction materials reads like a list of war preparations: 43,000 windows, or 600,00 square feet of glass; 200,000 tons of structural steel (more than was used for the Verrazano Narrows Bridge from Staten Island to Brooklyn); 6 acres of marble; 40,000 doorknobs; 200 elevators; 1,200 restrooms. Yamasaki was so used to small-scale projects that when he won the commission for the $280 million project, he thought it was simply a typo and that they meant $28 million.

The site was problematic because it was reclaimed river, and bedrock was 70 feet down. The engineers John Skilling and Leslie Robertson adopted an ingenious Italian technique called slurrying to build a solid foundation for the world's tallest buildings. As dirt and rock were removed, the pit was filled with slurry, a mixture of water and absorbent clay, to keep the excavation walls firm. Reinforced blocks of concrete were lowered into the slurry until they touched bedrock and then concrete was poured over them. The 500-square-foot foundation became known as "the bathtub" when it hardened. This engineering feat was also remarkable because the newly dug tunnels of the PATH

train to New Jersey stood exposed, five stories above bedrock, until the foundation was laid.

The World Trade differed from many of its glass-box contemporaries because it was supported by an external, rather than internal, steel-frame skeleton. The structure was essentially that of a rigid, hollow box, with load-bearing steel piers lashed together by the floor trusses, which extend to the central service core. In a widely imitated model, the elevators were distributed by sky lobbies with express elevators to the 44th and 78th floors. (The steel-and-drywall core could not withstand the heat from the explosions and was a major factor in the collapse.)

The most idiosyncratic aspect of the design was that the windows cover only 30 percent of the building's surface instead of the virtually all-glass façades of the International Style. The windows were only 18 inches wide, set between 18-inch-wide columns and sheathed in aluminum alloy that projected 12 inches from the surface of the glass. The spacing had as much to do with Yamasaki's fear of heights as with structural and design considerations. Apparently, the architect did not feel comfortable unless the floor-to-ceiling windows were narrower than his own shoulder span. Yamasaki wrote of his earlier Reynolds Building, "These relatively narrow windows offer magnificent views of the river and the city yet they give a sense of security and relieve the feelings of acrophobia that many people experience in high-rise buildings."

The major criticism of the complex was that it ignored the Manhattan skyline, but Yamasaki received the commission in part because of his thoughtful letter to the design board. "In my opinion, this should not be an overall form which melts into the multitiered landscape of Lower Manhattan," he wrote, "but it should be unique, have excitement of its own, and yet be respectful to the general area. The great scope of your project demands finding a

way to scale it to the human being so that, rather than be an overpowering group of buildings, it will be inviting, friendly and humane."

Despite their disregard for urban contextualism, the towers played off each other wonderfully as pieces of minimalist sculpture. Following the archetype laid out by Mies with his Lake Shore Drive Apartments (1948–51) in Chicago, Yamasaki staggered the towers so that the observer is always aware of their spatial relationships. One building appeared in the foreground with a lesser, perspectively distorted version behind it, so that the viewer was constantly confronted with the subjectivity of his viewpoint.

The customized aluminum-alloy skin, chosen by Yamasaki because it was warmer in tone than standard aluminum, was visually engaging as a reflector for the broad skies over Lower Manhattan. The chamfered corners gleamed with the same sense of limitless opportunities provided by the chrome-nickel alloy mullions of the Empire State Building. At sunset, the transparent glass cages became sculptural containers of space.

[1] The World Financial Center brought the World Trade Center towers back into the skyline.   [2] Tokens of commemoration of 9/11 line the Brooklyn Heights promenade, looking out over the harbor at the World Trade Center site.   [3] The lobbies were connected to a large underground shopping and commuter concourse.

One Liberty Plaza

(originally U.S. Steel Building)   ROY ALLEN OF SKIDMORE, OWINGS & MERRILL, 1974

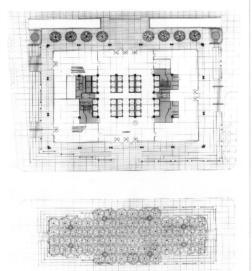

THE SKYWARD trend of thought," as the critic Thomas A. P. van Leeuwen refers to the evolution of skyscraper design, periodically hits a dead end and must be reimagined. The U.S. Steel Building is the endgame of Mies's reductionism, just as the 1915 Equitable Building catercorner across Broadway represents the exhaustion of the eclectic style. The two behemoths squaring off across Broadway have much in common; both buildings make no bones about being raw containers of office space through the sheer multiplication of layers.

The symbol of the New York headquarters of U.S. Steel is loud and clear: structural steel. The 150- by-250-foot trabeated slab, organized into three by five extraordinarily wide 50-foot bays, looks like a stack of steel girders, a solid promotion for U.S. Steel's principle product. The bays are spanned by heavily flanged, six-foot-deep steel-plate girders that act as spandrels. The structural frame and elevator core support the enormous, 40,000-square-foot floor plates without internal columns. Cass Gilbert would have appreciated how the U.S. Steel Building fulfills his definition of a skyscraper as "a machine that makes the land pay": each floor is almost an acre in area. The building is 53 stories and 772 feet tall, containing 1.8 million square feet of space.

This was the first New York skyscraper with exposed perimeter beams, but the façade is not completely honest. The structural steel had to be fireproofed, and the material was designed to be covered with another layer of steel so that the piers and the flanges of the spandrels appear even bigger. As a result, the rap of a knucklebone on one of the giant piers that runs straight up from the pavement gives a disconcertingly hollow sound, as if the building is an illusion. The strips of black window glass disappear into the deeply shadowed recesses of the skeletal façade. In a brilliant design gesture, the overscaled H-beam piers rise uninterruptedly to pierce the cornice line, as if the building could go on forever.

"This is not a glass building with a skeleton frame," noted the Museum of Modern Art's Arthur Drexler. "It is a steel building with glazed slots, hypnotically compelling, especially as the eye climbs the rungs of the façade and the glass disappears altogether." The sheer weight of the steel seems to press the tower down into its curious sunken plaza.

The tower was allowed to take up the bulk of the block bordered by Church, Corlandt, and Liberty Streets and Broadway in exchange for providing the pedestrian-only Liberty Plaza across the street, one in an archipelago of plazas that extends west from Chase Manhattan to Marine Midland to the World Trade Center. The respective towers stand in their squares like the last, lonely, kinged pieces on a checkerboard.

U.S. Steel is a well-conceived, if intimidating presence, similar to Skidmore, Owings & Merrill's aggressive work in Chicago during the same period. This type of muscular architecture works better in the city of the big shoulders, which has a more spread-out skyline than Manhattan.

The building's ownership reflects the vicissitudes of New York's economic base, from manufacturing to finance to real-estate shell game. Beset by shrinking domestic steel production, U.S. Steel sold the building to Merrill Lynch, which downsized in response to stock market declines and sold the building to the Canadian real-estate giant Olympia & York, which went spectacularly bankrupt. The building is currently owned by World Financial Properties, the considerably scaled-down reorganization of Olympia & York. Perhaps a building made of Cor-Ten, U.S. Steel's naturally weathering steel product that oxidizes to rust-brown, would be a more apt symbol of the American steel industry, which for the first time became an importer in the early 1980s.

[1] The U.S. Steel Building is a steel cage with glass slots, rather than a glass box   [2].A Chock Full o' Nuts coffee bar was a famous holdout on the open plaza, bottom.

1 and 2 UN Plaza

FIRST AVENUE AND EAST 44TH STREET » KEVIN ROCHE JOHN DINKELOO & ASSOCIATES, 1976 AND 1983

L I K E T H E Citicorp Center, the UN Plaza buildings are an early departure from the Internationalist aesthetic of structural expression. While Kevin Roche and John Dinkeloo's Ford Foundation (1963–68) two blocks away reveals the anatomy of a skyscraper, like a building turned inside out, their glass-sheathed UN towers are as cryptic as possible, like a man hiding behind mirrored sunglasses.

The blue-green skin, gridded with near-flush aluminum mullions, has the weightless, abstract quality of folded graph paper, or origami in glass. The surface tells you next to nothing about the building's internal steel cage construction. The aluminum grid does not correspond the interior floor levels—the horizontal 4-foot, 7-inch by 2-foot, 7.5-inch panels divide the floors into four—so there is no way of telling visually how tall the building is. The lack of scale is heightened by volumetric illusions. From some angles, the creases of the building are so

sharp that the planes of glass look perfectly two-dimensional. At night, when interior lights are on, the sudden perception of depth in a wafer-thin plane appears to be an optical illusion. At street level, the façade billows into an unsupported glass skirt that floats like a hydrofoil.

The buildings are marvelously responsive to atmospherics. Against a clear blue sky, the glass seems to dematerialize altogether, leaving only the gleaming grid of mullions so that the steel-cage is expressed after all, but in a refined and idealized way. The glaucous-colored glass looks different in shade and sunlight, adding a textured appearance. On overcast days, the mass of the building seems to simply drift off into the sky like trailing clouds. The tower forms play off of each other and the void of sky between them.

The towers recapitulate and extend the history of skyscraper design. The earlier, 39-story, 505-foot-tall No. 1 building is in the set-back tradition, with a recognizable podium, shaft, and crown, but the transitions are steeply

acute rather than orthogonal, highlighting their stylistic rather than structural role. No. 1 is quite anthropomorphic, with a "shoulder" and squarish head like a sphinx. There is a delicate contextualism for such large buildings: in color and structure, both towers are a tribute to their iconic neighbor, the UN Secretariat. The illusory scale of the grids is an indirect reference to the opaque glass panels on the north wall of the UN General Assembly. The 40-story No. 2 folds in at the corner up to its twelfth story, in deference to William Lescaze's high-modernist Church Peace Center (1962) at the corner of First Avenue and East 44th Street.

The mirrored interior is like a fun-house, fracturing space into planes of reflections, solids, and clear space. The beehive-pyramided reception area creates an infinity of mirrors and lights, a counterpart to the deceptions of the reflective façade. This is a postmodern update of the dark, faceted, Expressionist Chrysler and Daily News Buildings. There are a few modernist fantasy touches as well: a skybridge connects the towers, and there is a swimming pool on the twenty-seventh floor. More recently, Donald Trump has sewn together a package of air rights and zoning easements, and plans to build the world's tallest residential skyscraper, an 861-foot-tall glass tower, at First Avenue and 48th Street that would overshadow the Secretariat.

[1] The UN Secretariat and Plaza guard the East River waterfront.   [2] Unlike 1 and 2 UN Plaza, Roche and Dinkeloo's Ford Foundation Building at 320 East 43rd Street reveals the anatomy of a skyscraper.

Citicorp Center

LEXINGTON AVENUE BETWEEN EAST 53RD AND EAST 54TH STREETS » HUGH STUBBINS, 1978

1

THE 59-STORY, 915-foot-tall Citicorp Center, containing 1.3 million square feet, is sheathed in space-age aluminum and mirrored glass, and floats on 114-foot tall supercolumns. This is the city's first postmodern skyscraper, and it changed the playing field forever.

The Boston-based architect Hugh Stubbins violated two axioms of the Internationalist aesthetic in the construction of this building. The first was the absolute ban on applied symbolic decoration. The Citicorp's distinctive triangular top was the first purely decorative crown on a skyscraper since the Art Deco era. The crown had an ostensible function—it was intended to be a solar panel in the energy-conscious 1970s, but it was never used as such, and ultimately became simply a design expression. There was a ripple effect in the architecture world, like the discovery of the emperor's new clothes: flat tops were not an absolute verity after all, but simply another style among many to chose from. Citicorp laid the groundwork for

the fanciful variations of the 1980s and 1990s, such as Philip Johnson's Chippendale top for the AT&T Building, Helmut Jahn's ball-topped 750 Lexington Avenue (1987), and the faceted Louis Vuitton headquarters (1999) by Christian de Portzamparc on East 57th Street.

Citicorp is also a departure from the rule of strict structural expression. Just what holds this building up, anyway? The flush glass curtain wall with aluminum spandrels does not offer any clues. There is a bit of engineering legerdemain going on here: four supercolumns, flush with the sides but moved in and centered at 72 feet from the cantilevered corners, support the building along with the octagonal elevator core, which stands exposed in the center. Additional support is provided by the discreet bustle of the shopping mall in the rear, which functions like an anchorage on a suspension bridge to counteract the weight of the cantilevered structure.

The skyscraper was one of the first buildings in the world to use a tuned mass damper, a 400-ton, 30-foot-square, 8-½-foot-thick block

of concrete in the crown that slides on a thin layer of oil to convey its inertia to the building's structure under high-wind stress. The mass is "tuned" to counteract the oscillation of the swaying building, and reduces the motion by almost half. Diagonal windbraces, repeated on an eight-story module, run along the perimeter and are concealed by the skin. After Citicorp was built, an engineer discovered a fatal design flaw: the bolted joints were vulnerable to stress in the extremely high winds that occur once every 16 or so years in New York. Welders worked around the clock to add bolted, steel-reinforced plates over the joints.

The quality of public space here is quite good. Not since Rockefeller Center have such pleasant plazas and interior spaces been accessible from the subway. The steps leading from street level down to the main entrance double as seating, and Citicorp's open base makes the space seem more like a plaza than a pit at the foot of a skyscraper.

Citicorp exemplifies a fascinating transitional stage in postmodern design, because it embraces symbolism over structural expression, but still adheres to the unity of modernism in its lack of contextualism and its uniform style. The signage replaces traditional city lampposts and street signs, as if delivering a message from the future. Even the little corner newsstand is painted a futuristic silver.

[1] Citibank's slick exterior does not reveal the tower's structural secrets.

Trump Tower

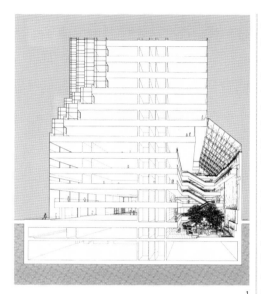

1

2

3

GLITZY" IS an adjective often applied to Scutt's work, and with all things glitzy—Liberace's wardrobe, Las Vegas, the Academy Awards— there is a strong component of kitsch, vulgarity, and glamour. Visitors come to Trump Tower to experience architecture in a way one does in few other spaces: they ride the escalators wide-eyed, heads atilt, video and flash cameras at the ready. The 58-story, 664-foot-tall tower's six-story atrium is a sensory overload.

Scutt learned his lessons from Las Vegas. His materials are sensuous to the point of giddiness: acres of glowing apricot Breccia Pernice marble (no wonder Italian quarrymen call marble *carne*, or "flesh"—there is a Rubenesque carnality to the whole interior). Flattering bronze mirrors reflect the surfaces into infinity. The detailing is exact, down to the bronze Chippendale-topped showcases capped with T's for Trump. Real-estate magnate Donald Trump is reified throughout, from awards on the wall to his personal books on display, like a latter-day Caesar.

The surface glamour almost gets in the way of perceiving what a fine postmodern space this is. The building is about surface or, more accurately, the interpenetration of surface and space. The skylit atrium is like a carnival hall of mirrors that splinters and refracts space. From any vantage point, it is not immediately clear what is solid surface, what is reflection, and what is space perceived through glass. The result is that the whole volume of interior space is pulled apart, and left that way, like open drawers in a chest.

Scutt does not try to impose a modernist unity on the space: it is fragmented and discontinuous in a way that buildings never were before. Structural columns disappear behind mirrored panels that make their support seem illusory. Escalator riders seem to float on air above mirrored panels, and appear fragmented and even headless from other angles. Modernists were always on the verge pulling space apart, but sought unity; Der Scutt is happy to leave space in pieces like the shards of a broken mirror. The disjunctive properties of the interior space are even clearer now that the atrium is connected by an interior passage in a postmodern collage to the oversized basketball gym of Niketown and the IBM Building courtyard nearby.

The bronze glass exterior is not quite as exciting, and may have contributed to the building's generally low critical rating. The façade sets back horizontally rather than vertically and cascades into a series of small, planted setbacks in the base. Philip Johnson and John Burgee used a similar technique in their streamlined glass Transco Tower in Houston, completed the same year.

[1] Trump residences are typically one-third empty, because the owners have multiple homes.　[2] The Trump's vertically aligned setbacks create a sawtooth profile against the sky.　[3] Inside: open vs. enclosed space, solids vs. voids, and reflected vs. transparent surfaces.

IBM Building

590 MADISON AVENUE » EDWARD LARRABEE BARNES, 1983

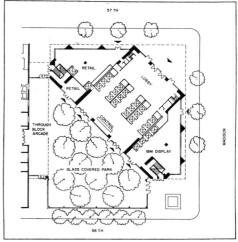

THE 43-STORY IBM Building is a transitional object between the self-imposed severity of high modernism and the new freedom of postmodernism. The building's principal deviations from Internationalist orthodoxy are in its use of materials and its daring lack of structural expression. Edward L. Barnes luxuriates in shape and color. The building is boldly sculptural rather than structural, a faceted, five-sided chunk of green-gray granite and glass, like a piece of the Emerald City of Oz. This is one of the more successfully lithic new buildings: the heavy cornice looks like solid stone, and the lobby corridors look as if they were mined out of a central core. Barnes was interested in symbolic rather than purely structural expression: the building corner that juts over Madison and 57th Street is wildly cantilevered.

"I think we're going through a rediscovery of the entranceway as a space of consummate importance," Mary Barnes, a designer for the firm and wife of Edward Larrabee Barnes, said

when the building was opened. "It is once again seen as a principal part of a building, one that draws attention to itself, draws the public in and has a life of its own."

The façade is organized into a flush curtain wall of alternating bands of continuous windows and granite spandrels that seem to float on top of one another. The subaqueous-colored windows make the building's skin look slick and solid, but lights shine through, showing that it is still a container of space.

Both the banded structure and the lithic quality of the building have roots in modern architecture, but their use at such a late stage makes them postmodern. The bands of windows that end in razor-thin mullions and make the building seem to float recall Frank Lloyd Wright's Johnson Wax Laboratory Tower in Racine, Wisconsin (1936–39), and the greenish stone skin evokes Raymond Hood's McGraw-Hill Building.

Despite these postmodern variations, the IBM remains strongly in the modern tradition,

because Barnes's principal interest was in unifying interior and exterior spaces. This is a wonderfully penetrable building. The granite paving sweeps through a glass-wrapped lobby. The mirrored ceiling in the triple-height lobby makes observers aware of the volume of space that surrounds them, and their relationship to the space. There is a sense of unity in the detailing: the floor indicators are floating bands of light, almost like a Donald Judd sculpture, which in turn echo the organization of the façade and the IBM logo itself. The 65-foot-high, 10,000-square-foot glass-walled atrium that borders on 56th Street unifies the interior with the street. Lobby, plaza, and street all flow into each other in the best traditions of Wright and Mies.

[1] The glass-enclosed atrium is one of the most successful public spaces in the city.   [2] The open lobby is accessible from many entrances.

AT&T Building

(now Sony Building) 550 MADISON AVENUE » PHILIP JOHNSON / JOHN BURGEE, 1984

As A critic who helped define the International Style, as Mies's associate architect on the Seagram Building, and as the designer of his own iconic Glass House (1949), Philip Johnson has impeccable high-modernist credentials. But his 42-story, rose granite–clad AT&T Building was designed specifically to stand all the received knowledge of Internationalism on its head.

Johnson deliberately made the decorative elements of the AT&T Building its most salient feature. With its overscaled, broken-pediment top and giant arched entryway, the AT&T was one of the most controversial buildings of the decade. Nobody had seen anything this aggressively postmodern on such a large scale before.

The brilliant formalist reversal of the scheme is that the decorative elements have true weight and heft, while the structure seems a bit two-dimensional and sketchy. The giant 34-foot-in-diameter keyhole oculus looks like a core sample was augered out of solid granite, and has more weight than the rather flimsy-looking shaft. The base features an overscaled Renaissance arch with a thickly articulated molding, heavier even than the skinny, continuous mullions.

The result is a shade cartoonish—a monumental top and a monumental base on a stretchy, hyperextended tower, set on an avenue so narrow that the viewer cannot even take in the whole thing at one time. "It was a normal thing to break the pediment somehow, though it is so much against the canons," Johnson recalled in his oral biography. "I had a classicist working for me at the time who said, 'You can't do that! You have to put back the molding.' That was fun and games for us." Some critics were less than amused, however. "It is a very funny place in which all of the grand gestures have gone foolishly or fatuously awry," Ada Louise Huxtable sniffed, "but one doubts this was the kind of wit the architects intended."

Or perhaps it was. There are a lot of interesting twists here. In many ways, despite its bizarrerie, this is a resolutely classicist building.

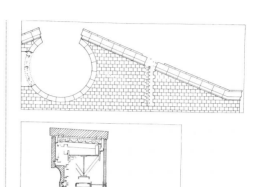

2

As Paul Goldberger noted at the time, "it is the only major skyscraper of the current generation in New York that will have floor plans of standard rectangular shape, instead of parallelograms or polygons." The individual parts, even if they do not make for an organic whole, stem from traditional sources: what is most often called the Chippendale top was inspired by Hadrian's arches in Asia Minor, and the colonnaded base recalls Rome's Palazzo Massimo, according to Johnson. "Idiosyncratic. Self-indulgent. Frivolous," scoffed the historian James Marston Fitch. "This preposterous design is perhaps a logical denouement for decades of increasingly mannered historicism." Johnson himself seemed delighted with the brouhaha. His name was once again in the vanguard of design, and people were talking passionately about architecture.

Some of the original design's monumentality was toned down by Sony, who leased the building in 1991. For example, *Genius of Electricity* (1916)—a gilded, 24-foot-tall statue of a winged man bearing lightning bolts and electrical cable by Evelyn Longman that topped the former AT&T headquarters at 195 Broadway—once dominated the 65-foot-high loggia under a gilded, cross-vaulted arch ceiling. The statue now resides at AT&T's operating headquarters in Basking Ridge, New Jersey. A 1994 remodeling by the firm Gwathmey Siegel turned the base's drafty, seldom-used, open arcade into a livelier, glassed-in, commodity-filled mall.

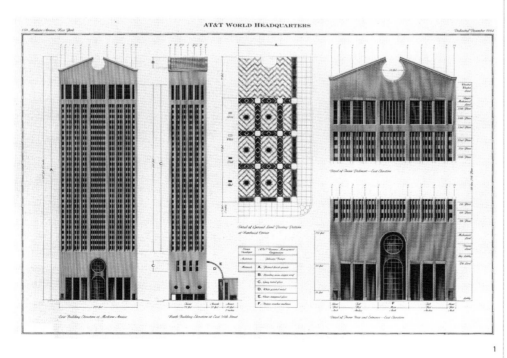

[1] These elegant elevation drawings reflect the tower's Renaissance origins.   [2] Johnson's once-controversial Chippendale broken pediment is now a familiar landmark.

Marriott Marquis Hotel

1531–1549 BROADWAY » JOHN PORTMAN, 1985

THE ARCHITECT and developer John Portman is best known for building destination points for cities that no longer had urban centers, such as Atlanta's Peachtree Center (1976) and Detroit's Renaissance Center (1977). His 54-story, H-shaped concrete slab is the closest thing New York has to the forbidding but interesting projects of the Italian futurist architects Antonio Sant'Elia and Mario Chiattone, with their multistoried blind walls. The building is situated in the bow tie of Times Square and epitomizes an era of urban planning. Although it is thoroughly un-New York in character, the building is fascinatingly effective taken on its own terms.

Planned in the mid-1970s, when Times Square's reputation was as its lowest, the whole building seems to turn its back defensively on the street. Like Ifill, Johnson & Hanchard's awesomely hostile Harlem State Office Building (1973), the Marquis shuns the street. "We knew we had to overcome the negative image of Times Square," Portman said, so he "created a design that looks to security, though not in a negative way." How negative is a matter of opinion; the

Marriott's soulless blank concrete wall is even less giving toward the street than its neighbor, One Astor Plaza. Between them, they create a concrete wind tunnel rather than a city block. From street level, the deeply recessed windows behind concrete sills seem to close up like a giant Venetian blind, an appropriate image for an overscale hotel of 1,900 rooms. Like the Mongols, who despised cities so much they tore them down stone by stone, the architects of the Times Square revival "created a desert and called it peace," in the words of historian Harold Lamb.

The detailing is ghastly—minimally textured concrete, rough edges, and bare bulbs stuck in gutters in keeping with the "show-biz" environment. But the antiurbanism here is insidiously brilliant—the entrance is not from the Broadway front, but from a pedestrian-unfriendly interior private road, so that it makes more sense to enter by car than on foot. The lobby was designed to filter out the unsavory mix of street life from Times Square: the 400-foot-high atrium, one of the tallest indoor spaces in the world, does not even begin until the eighth floor; and a glass-encased ground floor, dominated by a security desk, connects with the atrium via a series of escalators. The structure, though brutal, is directly expressed: a 112-foot steel truss joins two vertical, 36-foot-deep concrete-clad steel slabs.

"When you are in them, Portman's worlds are completely convincing," Vincent Scully noted, but this building has the same kind of

hermetic verisimilitude of the tritest science fiction sets, like *Logan's Run*. The building required so many zoning variations and easements in the course of its 12-year development that its style was already out of date by the time it was built. The atrium looks as if it was designed on laughing gas but provides the same pleasures as an amusement park: test-tube-shaped exposed glass elevators rocket up and down the vertiginously narrow space, disappearing through holes in the ceiling and floor. The city's only revolving restaurant is located here; there is also a revolving bar on the eighth floor, but it has no views worth speaking of. The series of exits from the 1,600-seat Marquis Theater, which supplanted three older theaters, is so complicated that it resembles a Rube Goldberg device. The exterior street level is sprouting new electronic signs like lichenous growths. As Rem Koolhaas wrote: "Since the Romans, the atrium had been a hole in a house or a building that injects light and air—the outside—into the center; in Portman's hands it became the opposite: a container of artificiality that allows its occupants to avoid daylight forever—a hermetic interior, sealed against the real.... With atriums as their private mini-centers, buildings no longer depend on specific location. They can be anywhere."

[1] Portman's Marquis Theater creates a sea of red plush.   [2] The Marriott Marquis's atrium evokes science-fiction imagery.   [3] A cross-section shows see-through elevators ascending to a revolving restaurant.

Lipstick Building

885 THIRD AVENUE » JOHN BURGEE WITH PHILIP JOHNSON, 1986

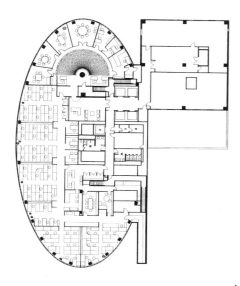

IN THE Lipstick Building, Philip Johnson put forth an even more heretical proposition than the assertion that applied symbolism was more interesting than structural expression: they dared to say that architecture was a game of passing styles, more akin to fashion than a search for perfect forms. Johnson began to refer to a building's exterior cladding as "heavy dress," implying that architectural style had no more real significance than hemline lengths. Such talk made the architects who were looking to add their designs to the canon of twentieth-century architecture nervous. But if fashion is so transient, why does the Lipstick work so hard to be a singularity?

The 36-story story, elliptical, dusty-rose glass and granite façade evokes the glamour of Art Deco. Immediately dubbed "the Lipstick" because of its three-tiered telescoping parti, the off-center tower recalls the smokestacks of a luxury steamship, but does not quite look like anything that came before it. The whole building has a nervous, unstable energy, a faster-motion version of the Flatiron's forward-looking modernism. The brushed steel bands of the wobbly façade catch the light like bangles on the arm of a woman making a hectic gesture at a party. Further, glass buildings were usually envisioned as faceted crystals, whereas this one is smooth; they are supposed to be light, while this one has the ponderousness of stone. Buildings are supposed to be enduring statements, but Johnson and Burgee seem to have chosen a nail-polish color from the mid-1980s and applied it to their façade, making it as much a period piece as Raymond Hood's sea-green McGraw-Hill Building.

From his offices on the sixteenth floor of the Lipstick, Johnson seems to have gone completely against his early manifesto with Henry-Russell Hitchcock, *The International Style* (1932), which grew out of their definitive exhibit at the Museum of Modern Art that same year. Instead of a smooth, continuous surface that expresses volume, the Lipstick has a bumptious, segmented curve that calls attention to itself not as a container of space, but as an irregular sculptural line. The principle of regularity, too, goes by the boards. The Lipstick's ellipsoidal ceilings are wildly impractical from the point of view of installing standardized lighting and ventilation fixtures. Discontinuity is emphasized at every level; the twinned columns at the base look ready to march off in different directions like giant soldiers from *The Nutcracker Suite*. The capitals do not quite seem to touch the lintels, which adds to the impression of instability.

"I'm a jumper-arounder anyhow," Johnson wrote in the foreword to the 1995 edition of *The International Style*. "Architecture's hold as art on professional and public intent is as precarious as it was in 1932." In his latest work, Johnson appears to be abandoning all notions of Euclidean geometry with his project for the boneless Peter Lewis Guest House (1995) in Lyndhurst, Ohio.

[1] The ellipsoidal floor plan added to the cost of lighting and HVAC installation.

425 Lexington Avenue

HELMUT JAHN, 1988

1

2

UNLIKE MANY postmodern architects, who seem burdened by the weight of history and stultified in trying to find some new wrinkle, the prolific Helmut Jahn appears to be enjoying himself. Some of the best examples of the German-born, Chicago-based architect's work are the bizarre, 17-story sliced-cylinder aerie of Chicago's State of Illinois Center (1985), and the joyously retro glass spire of Philadelphia's Liberty Place (1987). But there is a lot of Jahn's work in New York, including the 36-story Park Avenue Tower at 65 East 55th Street; the 69-story, 830-foot-tall, Moorish-domed CitySpire (1989) at 150 West 56th Street; and the 31-story 750 Lexington Avenue (1989). The latter, a mushroom-topped structure, is a very good building, especially considering its challenging site, and is highly representative of mid-1980s postmodernism.

The best part of 425 Lexington is its sense of play with historical forms. Jahn designed the building as a free-standing column, with a distinct podium, shaft, and cornice. However,

unlike eclectic buildings, the crown, which juts out at an angle over the sidewalk, is actually functioning office space. From inside, the occupants, should they choose, can look straight down the sheer face of the building. The silhouette that flares at the top has historical origins in the Palazzo Vecchio of 1314 in Florence, and fascinating postwar Milanese experiments such as Ernesto Nathan Rogers and Enrico Peressutti's Torre Velasca (1956–58).

Jahn's sly wit emerges in his dialogue with neighboring buildings. This is an architecturally rich and dense area: the Chrysler Building is just across the street, and the Citicorp Headquarters, the UN Plaza Buildings, and the UN Secretariat—all distinctive glass towers—are within sight. Jahn's work complements its predecessors: the blue-green glass is a tribute to the Secretariat, the massless folded glass planes evoke the UN Plaza towers, and the angled top is a variation on the Citicorp's perfect triangle top. Its chamfered, octagonal parti is a nod to the Pan Am Building.

Building a tower next door to perhaps the most famous and beloved skyscraper in the world could be a thankless task, but Jahn handles it graciously. He pays the Chrysler the ultimate compliment by simply mirroring it; 425 Lexington provides a life-size image of the Chrysler in its own reflective glass, with a kind of postmodern twist provided by the distortions in the glass itself. Jahn's crown supports rather than competes with the Chrysler's baroque spire, another subtle and generous gesture. The angled top of 425 echoes the angles of the urn-like radiator caps on the Chrysler at a similar height. The façade of 425 Lexington also recalls the Chrysler's organization of horizontally aligned framing corners and vertical central bays.

In other aspects 425 Lexington is very much a product of the late 1980s, with its overkill use of costly looking materials, and particularly in its rose and aqua coloring, the signature colors of the period. The triple-height, marble-lined lobby is vacuous but, once again, generous to its neighbors; the glass entryway nicely frames the Art Deco glories of the Graybar Building (Sloan & Robertson, 1927) across Lexington Avenue.

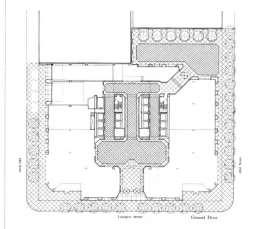

3

[1] The mid-1980s were marked by conspicuous consumption of stone and of space.   [2] The architect's sketches emphasize the façade's textural qualities.   [3] Retail space and a vast lobby wrap around the elevator core.

Worldwide Plaza

WEST 49TH TO WEST 50TH STREETS, BETWEEN EIGHTH AND NINTH AVENUES »

OFFICE TOWER, DAVID CHILDS; CONDOMINIUMS, FRANK WILLIAMS;

BOTH OF SKIDMORE, OWINGS & MERRILL, 1989

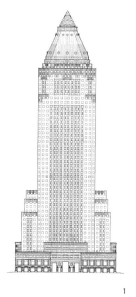

NINTH AVENUE

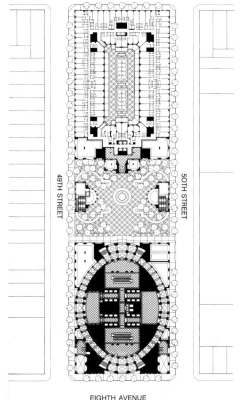

EIGHTH AVENUE

2

T OO MUCH complexity and contradiction can be exhausting. The mind, like a classicist, seeks integrated patterns in the world, and the task of breaking down patterns into their component pieces in order to decode them can be frustrating. Parts of Skidmore, Owings & Merrill's stone-clad, retro, 48-story, 770-foot-tall Worldwide Plaza are very good; the silhouette, too, is good, but it does not necessarily make as good a whole.

The tower has a splashy base and crown and a bloated shaft that looks better from far away on the skyline than close up. David Childs, the design architect, said he wanted to make his tower "the perfect example of what we all imagine around the world to be the great American classical skyscraper." Rather than just a high-rise, he wanted his building to have the panache of "the drum major in the Rockefeller band." The tower lacks Rockefeller Center's sweetly naïve spirit, yet still manages to be a distinctive presence on the midtown skyline.

The chief difference between Art Deco spires and their postmodern cousins is in the amount of sheer floor space. The Cities Service

Building, with its wasp-waisted shaft was truly the last of its kind before the Depression; after World War II, the squat 100 Park Avenue became the model. Postmodernists synthesized the two, to make fat, blocky, setback skyscrapers that do not sacrifice any floor space for the sake of design. Childs's Worldwide Plaza contains acres of space, from the vacuous, Mussolini-scaled lobby to the fatuous subway "improvement" that provides picture windows with nothing more to show than the tiled hole of the subway entrance three stories below grade.

The building's best feature is its elliptical, barrel-vaulted pedestrian loggia at the base, evocative of the Renaissance, although on a grander scale. The shaft of maize- and rust-colored patterned brick above the granite-sheathed platform is organized into an overly fussy rhythm of one and two window bays, but the setbacks are appealingly decorated with lighter brick, like snowcaps. The payoff comes at the last setback, when the double bays are deeply recessed to form an arcade reminiscent of Trowbridge & Livingston's monumental Bankers Trust Company Building (1912), and especially Cass Gilbert's stout New York Life Insurance Company Building (1928), which served as an overall inspiration for Childs. It appears that the designers took real joy in the ornamental, internally lit, glazed pyramid atop a steeply sloped copper crown. At night, with the carminative mists emanating from the HVAC system, the building has the drama of a rocket ready for liftoff.

The complementing, 38-story condominium tower on the south side of the plaza by Frank Williams of Skidmore, Owings & Merrill is as open and glassy as the Worldwide is lithic. The tower's window corners end in thin steel mullions, where the clear blocks alternate with the solid ones. The building scales itself down nicely to the surrounding low-lying neighborhood of Clinton with five-story mansionettes that match the tenements across the street in height. Even a decade later, the gentrifying effect has not quite taken hold, and much of the retail space here, the site of the second Madison Square Garden of A. J. Liebling's day, is still vacant.

[1] The Worldwide's shaft is proportionally broader than in eclectic skyscrapers. [2] An overscaled Renaissance rotunda. bottom, is one of the site's best features. [3] The crown reflects the glamour of earlier eras.

1585 Broadway

(originally Solomon Equities Building)

GWATHMEY SIEGEL AND ASSOCIATES, 1990

2

1

ONCE THE modernist aesthetic of unity and structural expression was abandoned as yet another historical style, rather than the irreducible essence of architecture, architects adopted an "a-little-bit-of-everything" approach. Gwathmey Siegel's first skyscraper is one of the more successful, because seeing the building from different vantage points makes you perceive it differently.

The 52-story office tower's graphic façade of blue-green glass, white patterned glass, mirrored glass, silvery gray aluminum, and stainless steel can be read in many different ways, depending on light and atmosphere. It is both reflective and transparent, giving an illusion of metallic solidity and glassy evanescence. Details of the façade, such as the curved aluminum midsection and the corners tipped with mirror glass, catch and reflect sunlight. The building refuses to be perceived as a coherent whole, in keeping with the disjunctive aesthetic of postmodernism, and the jittery, electronic character of the Times Square area.

The cornice of the platform is defined by three amber-colored, 157-foot-long zip strips that flash stock quotes. Pixellated advertisements play on corner billboards, another step toward the electronic architecture anticipated in films like *Blade Runner*. In reaction to the Internationalists' suppression of applied symbolic elements, façades are now verging on pure symbolism in the form of electronic information.

The tower has a sleek, hide-and-seek structure, with massive framing piers at street level, but nearly invisible mullions in the tower. One scans the restless façade the same way one tries to decipher meaning from the cascading financial figures of the zip strip. (In the early 1990s, architectural historian Robert A. M. Stern and graphic designer Tibor Kalman were retained by the State Urban Development Corporation to set a special zoning code for the scale and location of all new signage in the area to preserve some of Times Square's carnivalesque atmosphere.)

The building is organized into three main sections, with its platform oriented toward the diagonal of Broadway. A blind, curved, mechanical floor of heating and ventilation grilles paneled in shiny aluminum facilitates the transition to the office tower, which is laid out orthogonally along the street grid. Shallow setbacks at the crown evoke Art Deco skyscrapers. Only from a distance does the sloping, ornamental roof spring into view to provide a distinctive silhouette.

The grand, through-block lobby provides one of those great disjunctive postmodern moments. In contrast to the flashy mutability of the façade, the interior materials are solid and luxurious. The glossy black, white, and green marble floor echoes the tricky gridded patterns of the façade. A deeply coffered wood ceiling adds a modernist sense of warmth to the space. The detailing of the overall motif of circles in squares is excellent, from the shiny metal disks under the revolving doors to the round structural columns and the circular light fixtures set in wood coffers.

[1] Cross sections.   [2] The disjuncture of the unified interior and the fragmented exterior is itself postmodernist.

Bertelsmann Building

(originally 1540 Broadway)

SKIDMORE, OWINGS & MERRILL, 1990

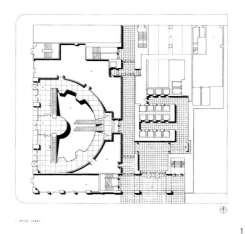

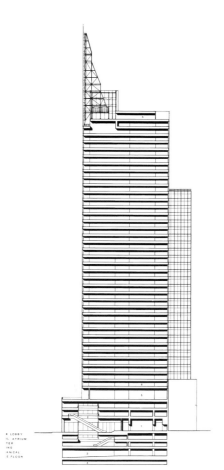

1 OFFICE LOBBY

R LOBBY
IL ATRIUM
TER
ING
ANICAL
E FLOOR

1

2

EVER SINCE Times Square became the city's entertainment district, its lure has been densely packed public space for people watching, and a kinetic cavalcade of electronic pop art in the form of advertising signs. Discontinuity and bricolage existed before French deconstructionism; it just took postmodern philosophy to elevate them to an aesthetic. With postmodernism, architects no longer felt they had to unify a building's image; the 45-story Bertelsmann Building presents different, and unrelated, faces.

From the uptown side, the Bertelsmann resembles a classic Internationalist aquarium, with its grid of flush, opaque, green glass-covered spandrels and green-tinted windows connected by aluminum mullions. This orientation is in keeping with the more business-like neighborhood of upper Sixth Avenue. The hypermodern façade seems to terminate next to a row of low dingy brick buildings, but this is illusory: the main entrance on Broadway sneaks around behind them, preserving the block's clutter and discontinuity. On the south façade, an extruded black glass sheath appears to contain squares of a lighter glass building within, and the top ends in strangely overscaled parapets. The blank podium of the entrance maintains the cornice line of Herts & Tallant's ornate Lyceum Theater (1903) next door, the city's oldest surviving legitimate playhouse.

The Broadway front is dominated by a triangular bay that ends in a skeletal, deconstructionist pinnacle that hearkens back to such visionary experiments as Vladimir Tatlin's project for the Monument to the Third International of 1919–20, which resembled the Cyclone at Coney Island. Skidmore, Owings & Merrill cannily presents the exposed scaffolding of a billboard as the image of a Times Square skyscraper. The bare crown reflects the busy ground level: they are the same, except for the veneer of billboards. The podium dissolves in a jumble of signs but the sign with the building's name forms a traditional cornice line.

Like Trump Tower, the interior is a shopping mall by any other name, but it is a good one. Here, deconstructionist architecture is used for its entertainment value, an appropriate motif for the multimedia Tower Records store: the three-level, 140,000-square-foot underground space is carved into unusual angles and ellipses, under a ceiling exposed to look like the lighting grid of a stage set. Structuralism is treated as an illusion; the supports change from square, marble-clad pillars to round, plaster-covered columns as they change levels. What looks like a major structural core covered in stainless steel turns out to be a hollow kiosk from another angle. Even the escalators are sided with glass to reveal their inner workings.

3

[1] This plan was modified to put the movie theater two stories underground.   [2] An early version of the atrium, which is now almost entirely below grade.   [3] The Bertelsmann building at night.

712 Fifth Avenue

KOHN PEDERSEN FOX, 1991

MID-1980s postmodernism drew attention to itself by not looking remotely like anything else around it. But by the early 1990s, Kohn Pedersen Fox's 712 Fifth Avenue was so tastefully contextual that it is easily overlooked. The designers seem to have swallowed an architectural history textbook whole, and integrated nearly all the surrounding buildings in their slender 55-story marble- and limestone-clad campanile.

The tower is set back 55 feet from the avenue in order to preserve the grand façades of Harry Winston diamonds on the corner, and the former Rizzoli bookstore and Coty cosmetics buildings (now Henri Bendel couture). Bendel was the jewel that preservationists fought to save, because its Art Nouveau etched-glass windows from 1913 are New York's only example of architectural glass by the French designer René Lalique. William Pedersen of Kohn Pedersen Fox devised a way to preserve the swank French

maison by connecting it as an entrance to 712 Fifth's lobby, and Beyer Blinder Belle revamped the store interior with a four-story atrium of marble and French limestone.

The façade of 712 Fifth takes its keynote from the small, elegant boutiques at its base. The lattice-work mullioned windows in the tower's central bays reflect Bendel's delicately-mullioned shop front, and the materials of Indiana limestone and white Vermont marble are a tribute to the luxe retail shops on Fifth Avenue. The longer one looks at 712 Fifth's façade, the more it seems to pick up elements of every building around it. Aren't those gilded spandrels a part of the Crown Building across the street, and don't the courses of rock-faced granite look like the venerable brownstone exterior of the Fifth Avenue Presbyterian Church on the corner? Even the top, with is flat stone crown divided into planes, seems to refer to Edward Durell Stone's GM Building and Gordon Bunshaft's 9 West 57th Street. The two-in-one façade of 712 Fifth looks right at home with the gray limestone of Rockefeller Center in the background, and the marble front of Bergdorf Goodman in the foreground.

At street level, the cornice of 712 Fifth's entrance on West 56th Street fits in unobtrusively with the established four- and five-story cornice line. Etched glass figures of the zodiac above the entrance echo the Lalique glass. The "baby grand" lobby is a minor letdown because of its diminutive scale, but there are some nice historicist references, such as the customized, mirror-finish mail chute.

The tower's concrete tube structure seems to float masslessly overhead, partly because it is set so far back from the street as to appear a little unreal, and because its flush skin and narrow proportions negate its volume, so that it appears as a dimensionless plane. The mirror windows further dematerialize the façade by making it an abstract grid against the sky. The façade accomplishes the seemingly contradictory tasks of

appearing weightless yet providing a textured play of light and shadow with subtle articulations in the depths of the windows. The different reflective properties of glass and stone make 712 Fifth succeed as both a foreground and a background building. The palette is subtly colorful, with accents of polished black and thermal green granite. Paradoxically, the detailing makes the big building feel like a Persian miniature.

William Pedersen has written that he seeks an architecture that "attempts to combine simultaneously the formal with the informal, the figural with the abstract, the monumental with the human, and the modern with the traditional," in a state of what Robert Venturi calls "difficult unity."

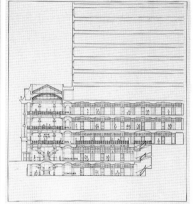

[1] The tower synthesizes all the elements of the block front five-story atrium, left   [2] The façade integrates seamlessly with Bendel's

World Financial Center

WEST STREET BETWEEN LIBERTY AND VESEY STREETS » CESAR PELLI, 1985–92 AND 2004

ESAR PELLI designed the $50 million renovation of his World Financial Center, which was heavily damaged in the attack on the World Trade Center. The rehaul required 2,000 new skylight panes and 1.2 million pounds of Italian and Spanish marble. The 10-story, 145-foot-high domed atrium of the Winter Garden is once again a venue for concerts and other public events under the palms.

The courtly, Argentinean-born Cesar Pelli, who was the dean of Yale's graduate department of architecture, uses postmodernism as an evolution rather than a negation of modernism. The four blunt towers of his World Financial Center, which range in height from 34 to 51 stories, recap and extend the development of skyscraper style.

The setback façades recount the history of the skyscraper. Each tower is divided into five major sections. The platforms appear to be largely lithic, with windows punctuating a granite-framed façade, evoking the first masonry skyscrapers. The proportions of stone and glass change at the setbacks. At the second setback the balance of stone and glass is more even, recalling the regularity of Rockefeller Center and its extension west of Sixth Avenue. The third setback before the attic is more open and glassy, with only the thinnest grid of superimposed granite mullions, resembling postwar high-modernist skyscrapers. At the very top stories, the form of the pure glass cube emerges, like Skidmore, Owings & Merrill's flush glass towers, but Pelli caps these with ornamental copper crowns in the form of a simple pyramid, a stepped-back pyramid, a dome, and a mastaba.

The setback heights at the 3rd, 9th, and 24th floors were determined by the New York State Urban Development Council, so that the complex would relate to the predominant building heights of Lower Manhattan. Pelli's towers are wittily contextual: the mastaba atop the 40-story-tall No. 1 is a visual echo of the mansard roof of Cass Gilbert's West Street Building

1

across the street. The orthogonal shaft of No. 3 is torqued on its irregular base, like the influential modernist parti of Ralph Walker's cater-corner Barclay-Vesey Building. "The city is more important than the building," Pelli said. "The building is more important than the architect. I connect with what is strongest in each place."

Pelli's towers reveal themselves to be layers of buildings, or buildings within buildings. He refers to the levels of cladding as "jackets." The setbacks also penetrate inward, like missing cake slices, revealing the core structure of glass and steel beneath the granite. The façades balance contradictory elements; corner pillars that

appear to be square blocks of granite stand revealed from another angle as thin façades covering round steel columns. All three stages of the illusion are revealed in one vista: fully sheathed column, column standing beside façade, and fully exposed column. Similarly, flush windows appear next to windows with deeply punched reveals, each negating the validity of the other: Is the granite wall thick and weight-bearing, or a mere screen? Pelli's contribution is to make structure and nonstructure appear as part of a unified, modernist-inspired continuum. However, critic Vincent Scully called the result "bulbous chunks bloated with rentable floor space. At the same time, they are thin and brittle in surface, because

[1] The Winter Garden, at center, now restored, a glass-enclosed atrium housing a baroque marble staircase and live Mojave palm trees, is the heart of the complex.

5

1

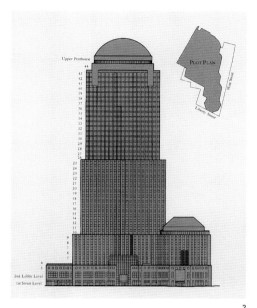

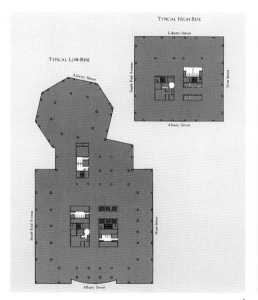

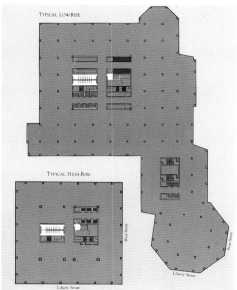

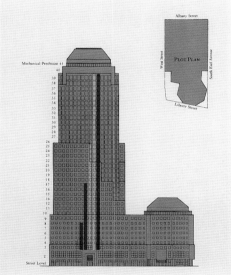

2

3

4

5

Pelli believes that only curtain walls are economically viable. There is a running argument as to whether or not he is right."

Pelli finds a synthesis in the protostructuralism of Victorian glass-and-steel architecture, which he demonstrates as the foundation of modern and postmodern architecture. The heart of the complex is the glass-enclosed Winter Garden. This organiform, Art Nouveau-esque atrium is 125 feet high, 120 feet wide, and 200 feet long, for a total of 18,000 square feet. A baroque marble staircase spills into a court lined with "living columns" of Mojave palm trees. Some modernist mythology is amazingly durable: this is the garden under glass of the Victorian hothouse, with a direct lineage through Raymond Hood's hanging gardens at Rockefeller Center, Roche & Dinkeloo's glass-encased Eden of the Ford Foundation Center, and the atrium of Edward Larrabee Barnes's IBM Building. The World Financial Center also has a dock for luxury yachts, one of which even has a helicopter on its top deck for quick escapes.

The Winter Garden is a tribute to Joseph Paxton's Crystal Palace, built for London's Great Exhibition of 1851. Paxton, a gardener by training, produced the prototype of all glass-and-steel architecture to follow with his three-tiered, over-scaled hothouse, which featured a flush glass perimeter. This is the basis of modern architecture, Pelli says; the rest is just various states of dress or undress. Pelli's essentially Victorian leanings in the World Financial Center are also revealed in the choice of fabric applications, which recall the designs of William Morris.

The different reflective properties of the materials in the towers give the visual effect of a skyline in miniature. At sunset, the stone base darkens before the towers. Interior lights shine from the stone base, while the glassier mid-section reflects the last rays of color, and the pure glass tops gleam like distant towers. This is a reference to the roots of the stone skyscraper in the Gothic cathedral, where the concept was to present an image of the entire city of heaven.

[1] The World Financial Center's waterfront park remains a playground for yachtsmen.   [2] The elevations recap the skyscraper's evolution in their proportions of stone to glass.   [3] The spread-out footprint of No. 2 provides maximum floor space.   [4] The footprint of No. 1 features a partial octagon.   [5] No. 1 is topped by a mastaba, an Egyptian tomb structure.

Four Seasons Hotel

57 EAST 57TH STREET » I. M. PEI, 1993

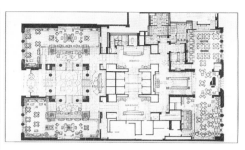

MANY ARCHITECTS saw post-modernism as a return to romance. I. M. Pei, who worked within an exacting minimalist lexicon for much of his career, let out the more playful side of his character with the Four Seasons Hotel. As a young student in China, Pei was impressed by the construction of the 23-story Art Deco Park Hotel in Shanghai, an event that inspired his decision to become an architect. Pei had skyscraper daydreams early in his career, like his unrealized project for a helical tower in New York that looked remarkably like the Capitol Records Building (1956) in Hollywood.

His 52-story, 682-foot-high Four Seasons Hotel, the tallest hotel in New York, captures the romance of a Josef von Sternberg film set for *Shanghai Express*. The $360-million, 367-room hotel features some of the most expensive suites in the city with panoramic views from the top floors. The ceiling heights are more than 10 feet. The top-of-the-line room—the 3,000-square-foot, two-bedroom presidential suite—costs $10,000 a night.

The setbacks of warm Magny de Louvre limestone are demarcated with 12-foot-high lanterns, which add drama to the sleek setbacks at night. The base is dominated by a hollow, over-scale symbol: a giant ox-eye window framed by a shallow light court—this symbol qua symbol, like the AT&T's Chippendale top, has no referent outside of itself, and is meant to be a visual landmark. A steel and frosted glass canopy cantilevers over the square-arched, 28-foot-wide entrance.

"This was Pei's attempt to make a big urban skyscraper," carped detractors such as Robert A. M. Stern. "It comes off as overbearing. A hotel should be a delightful place, not an exalting experience. It's just vulgar in my view with all those cheap jewel-like lights." But the usually self-effacing Pei, known for his mouse gray suits and brown shoes, is smarter than that. The Four Seasons is slyly contextual. It takes a while to appreciate how well the building fits

into 57th Street, and how it sums up skyscraper development. The obelisk-shaped lanterns recall the parti of the Ritz Tower down the street, the world's first residential skyscraper, and evoke a sense of shelter appropriate for a hotel. Alternating flush and recessed windows add texture to the façade, and there are a few anachronistic symbols of domesticity, such as molded windowsills punctuated with Edwardian drip-stones, in keeping with the boldly superfluous gesture of the ox-eye motif. From certain angles, the Four Season's slender shaft, almost unornamented except for its chamfered corners, is remarkably similar to the Fuller Building next door, reflecting the Fuller's Deco glamour. On the top floor of the Four Season's east and west elevations, there are even small, three-sided bay windows that echo the Fuller's balconies. The faceted crown evokes the mansarded Pierre Hotel down the avenue, and celebrates the joy of a sculptural object in sunlight.

The monumental, cubic 32-foot-square by 33-foot-tall lobby feels like a not entirely benign stage set, maybe from a retro-fascist future such as that in *Brazil*. A ceremonial Mussolini-esque reception desk with giant Art Deco lamps is elevated by six steps, more like a desk for a High Inquisitor than hotel staff. Octagonal columns that repeat the chamfered exterior reach up to the softly luminescent, backlit onyx ceiling. The walls are lined in limestone and mellow Danish beechwood. The net effect of the interior is oddly subdued, like the peristyle and hortus of a classical Roman house.

[1] This rendering echoes elements of neighboring towers, including the Fuller, the Ritz, and the Pierre.   [2] Interior and exterior surfaces are integrated with matching French limestone.   [3] The reception desk, center, is ceremonially raised above the hotel's sunken forecourt.

LVMH Building

L OUIS VUITTON MOËT HENNESSY'S 24-story, 328-foot-tall American flagship tower—part boutique, part office headquarters, and seemingly part iceberg—is not tall as skyscrapers go, but nonetheless has a great impact on the cityscape. Like a Gothic cathedral, whose myriad turrets and finials are meant to suggest a vision of the city of heaven, the LVMH looks like an entire skyline in miniature. The tricky folds and slices of its glass curtain wall provide an illusion of much greater height, so that it vies with older skyscraper neighbors like the Fuller Building across Lexington Avenue.

Even though the site is only 60 by 100 feet, the building's footprint is irregular and set back from the street line. The glass walls angle inward invitingly. Slender as a Parisian runway model with a nipped-in waist at the 11th floor, the tower has a distinctly feminine silhouette. French architect Christian de Portzamparc

found an unusual solution to the city's long-standing zoning code—after the setback, the glass wall cants outward at a five-degree angle to create a little extra floor space for the notoriously compact office. The tower at first seems radically noncontextual, but its jewel-like, faceted façade makes sense as a symbol for the luxury goods produced by the owner. It also succeeds as an emblem of 57th Street, one of the most expensive retail corridors in the world. A glowing diamond building does not look out of place near the granite vault of Tiffany's. The façade even contains a gem—a small, angled blue glass box at the setback.

The two-story base, unified by a shiny metal belt course emblazoned with the Dior label, consists of two boutiques that would not be out of place in the Paris or Berlin of the 1920s. The tower is difficult to take in all at once because its sweeping zigzag edges take the eye in all directions, but it is essentially divided into three major sections atop the stores. Each section is distinguished by the use of a different type of glass. The turret to the west is of light green glass made opaque with particles of ceramic, the irregularly angled east side consists of sand-blasted translucent glass and clear panes etched with narrow horizontal lines, while the main tower above the setback at the 11th floor is of a more traditional International Style dark green glass, befitting an office headquarters.

A single bay of windows on the east side slopes back vertiginously like a ski jump, so that the main setback and the neighboring buildings seem to loom over the observer like the set of an Expressionist film. The angled outline of the main setback and the fact that it tilts out slightly exaggerate the perspective of traditional vanishing points, so that it seems to taper off into celestial distances. The heavy cornice also swoops down to make a giant figure seven across the building, emphasizing the vertical sweep.

Like the more traditional Lever House, the LVMH dares to "waste" a lot of its air rights to

create a startling contrast between the building and the volume of space surrounding it. This factor, perhaps more than any other, turns de Portzamparc's design into a true skyscraper in miniature.

De Portzamparc has realized a German Expressionist vision of Glasarchitektur—a phantasmagoric, crystalline jewel lit from within. At night the grid and windows disappear, and facets of the building glow in cool shades of green. This makes the LVMH a tribute to the ambitions of great Deco skyscrapers like the Cities Service Building (70 Pine St.) and the Chrysler Building to create a cityscape that appeals to the visual imagination.

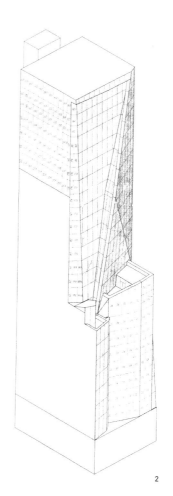

[1] The glass silhouette of the LVMH tower is as delicate as that of a Parisian runway model.   [2] Intricate folds of glass give the 24-story tower an illusion of greater height.

Times Square Buildings

NEW YORK'S Urban Development Corporation's plan for Times Square called for four antiurbanistic office towers by Philip Johnson and John Burgee to stand guard like cops on the beat over what was viewed as a squalid street scene. A subsequent plan, known as "42nd Street Now!" and created by a consortium of state, city, and private groups under the stewardship of Robert A. M. Stern and the graphic designer Tibor Kalman, prevailed in 1993 and turned Times Square into a tourist-friendly, themed outdoor mall.

The plan worked, for better or worse. Visitors have returned in droves to the eye-popping, Las Vegas–like blocks radiating from the bowtie of Times Square, bedizened with all manner of Jumbotrons and "spectaculars," as billboards with special effects are called in the trade. Even locals can sometimes only gaze agape at the carnival.

The scheme of four towers was replaced with four postmodern skyscrapers that cater to the neighborhood's eclectic nature. The buildings are all taller and more capacious than the original Johnson-Burgee designs, but are much more integrated into the street.

The 48-story, 809-foot-tall Condé Nast Building presents a "collage of visual experiences," in the words of architect Bruce S. Fowle. There are two main experiences: a curvilinear glass tower that faces the intersection of Times Square and a more sober-sided granite façade that presents itself to Manhattan's traditional business core to the south and west. The effect is best seen from a great distance when the shaft's smart, silvery skin glistens like a marlin's scales. From far west on 42nd Street, the two distinct sections appear like parts of a well-integrated cityscape.

1

[1] The collage of the Condé Nast Building reflects the hyperkinetic quality of its environs.

The element of showmanship is satisfied at street level on the northwest corner with the NASDAQ drum, a 90-by-120-foot video screen wrapped around a circular extension of the office building, with windows peeping surrealistically through the surface. When images sweep across the screen, the whole building seems to be in motion, an example of what Robert Venturi calls "iconography and electronics upon a generic architecture."

Despite its show-biz exterior, the interior uses a large amount of "green" technology. Spandrels at the upper level contain photovoltaic cells to generate up to 5 percent of the building's energy load, and the windows are treated to block heat from sunlight to lessen the burden on the cooling system.

1

[1] The Condé Nast cafeteria is the only example of the work of Frank Gehry in New York City. Unfortunately, it is not open to the public.   [2] The riot of colors in the Reuters Building reflects the kaleidoscope experience of Times Square.   [3] The glass lobby lets in the kaleidoscope of Times Square.

2

3

The 30-story, 486-foot-high Reuters Building makes a less clean distinction between its parts and so is harder to take in as a whole. Each side of the nearly freestanding, dullish-bronze glass tower presents a different face, but there is little dialog between façades.

The corner facing Times Square is glass-walled with a circular drum, but it has strange little bundled columns that would be more appropriate on the nearby Knickerbocker Hotel, a fin-de-siècle landmark. A giant wedge that slices perpendicularly through the top, intended as a show stopper, comes as little surprise on a street where a giant golden hand dangles over Madame Tussauds. Broadway is a tough act to follow.

On the north stands a granite setback with flush glass windows, a sign that Reuters means business. Fox & Fowle will soon have a trifecta in Times Square with a multisectioned, 35-story 11 Times Square opposite the Port Authority.

Kohn Pedersen Fox's 40-story, 575-foot Ernst & Young Building is built in the spirit of the other two towers, but has fewer ideas at play. The applied iconography is less splashy (no Jumbotrons). Interestingly, KPF arrived at the parti of two sections split by a beam of white light, independent of that at the Westin New York at Times Square by Arquitectonica. Perhaps both were an homage to the notion of the Great White Way.

This is a traditional brand of postmodernism. Diagonally sliced metal spandrels seem to etch a glass triangle on the façade, and a wraparound glass sheath twists at an odd angle. Unfortunately, there is not enough tension or dialectic between the parts, which is what makes other postmodern designs interesting.

With his boxy, 47-story, 726-foot-tall Times Square Tower, David Childs is on the verge of becoming the postmodern equivalent of the ubiquitous 1960s architect Emery Roth as New York's premier packager of commercial space. The tower takes advantage of a zoning exclusion and rises without setbacks to provide maximum square footage.

[1] The 30-story Reuters Building stands in front of the 40-story Ernst & Young Building. [2] David Child's 7 Times Square made use of a special zoning allowance so that it could rise straight up for 47 stories without setbacks to maximize the interior space.

175

Trump World Tower

845 UNITED NATIONS PLAZA » COSTAS KONDYLIS, 2002

WHEN THE developer Donald Trump announced that he was planning to build the world's tallest residential building next to the United Nations, local residents understandably feared it would obstruct views and overwhelm the neighborhood. The initial renderings certainly looked threatening: a glitzy, bronze-skinned slab that stood out like a nouveau-riche arriviste against the staid older buildings of Turtle Bay and Sutton Place and outshone the iconic UN Secretariat.

Then came the argument over just how tall the city was going to allow the Trump World Tower to be. Civic groups like the Municipal Art Society—who tend to like the city the way it is, or, better yet, as it used to be—tried to put a cap on the building's height even as steel was being set in the ground. Local residents, including Walter Cronkite, railed publicly that the building would block their million-dollar river views, which it ultimately did.

Trump craftily cobbled together what are called "transferable development rights," buying up air rights of seven surrounding properties, including the Japan Society and the Holy Family Catholic Church. A bonus height addition for creating a public plaza at the base allowed Trump to reach his goal—a 72-story, 863-foot tall tower. Trump originally touted the building

as 90 stories tall, because that would be its height if the floors were the conventional height of 8 feet. Some of the Trump apartments are prewar scale with maid's rooms, floor-to-ceiling windows, and unusually luxurious 10- to 16-foot ceiling heights. For two years, the Trump World Tower reigned as the tallest all-residential tower in the world, until it was surpassed by the 883-foot-tall 21st Century Tower in Dubai, United Arab Emirates.

If one can say such a thing about a Trump production, the design by the New York architect Costas Kondylis is reticent rather than brash. The curtain wall is a deep bronze, appearing almost black under overcast skies, so that the freestanding tower recedes and blends into the East River skyline instead of overpowering it.

The Trump World Tower provides an interesting contrast to New York's earlier skyscraper apartments such as the Ritz Tower and the San Remo Apartments by Emery Roth. The super-rich have long since abandoned attempts to display status through the trappings of a classical past, in favor of modernism's minimalist aesthetic. In a city as dense as New York, space and spectacular views are status symbols.

The construction is unusual in that the building is framed in extra-high-strength, reinforced concrete that does not require the added width of steel beams, allowing for greater height

between the floors. The all-concrete construction method allowed the building to go up in a mere 18 months, cutting down on construction costs and perhaps circumventing community opposition at the same time. Anchored in bedrock two stories below the ground, 27 concrete columns outline the perimeter of the base, lessening in number as the height increases. The columns are lashed together with a full-story concrete "belt" midway that creates a tube around the outside of the columns. A similar concrete band at the top provides lateral strength. At the crown, a 600-ton damper mass that responds by computer to wind forces gives the tower stability in high winds; this is the first such system to be used in a residential building.

Set atop a broad, two-story base, the tower rises without setbacks, with its broad side along the axis of the riverfront to maximize views and harmonize with the alignment of the UN Secretariat. The most appealing aspects of the slab are its dark-bronze, ultra-slick skin and its daringly narrow proportions. It is one of the slenderest towers in the city, and its great height only serves to exaggerate the effect.

The glass skin is one of the sheerest walls in New York, outside of Gordon Bunshaft's Marine Midland Bank Building at 140 Broadway. Except for a barely traced grid of silicon seams between the panes, the sleek skin appears to be a single sheet of glass towering two-dimensionally over the observer. The uncompromising smoothness of the surface, its stark verticality, and its narrowness give the slab the integrity of a minimalist object.

Kondylis, who has designed about 50 buildings in New York, says the Trump World Tower is his own tribute to the tower-in-a-plaza model of Mies van der Rohe's Seagram Building. Its dark color works well with the atmospherics Mies predicted for glass towers, reflecting patterns of clouds and light on sunny days, looking somber and impenetrable on overcast days, and blending with the romantic lights of the city by night. Traditional rather than innovative, Kondylis's flat-topped slab is an elegant wafer.

[1] Trump World Tower provides floor-to-ceiling views and extra high ceilings.

Austrian Cultural Forum

11 EAST 52ND STREET » RAIMUND ABRAHAM, 2002

1

LIKE THE LVMH BUILDING, the Austrian Cultural Forum presents both a vertical impact disproportionate to its height and a novel solution to the setback zoning code. Built on a miniscule 25-foot-wide, 81-foot-deep midblock site meant for a townhouse, Raimund Abraham's design aggressively breaks the vertical row of the street front with its massive, sloping planes.

The 24-story, 280-foot-tall infill building is ferociously uncompromising. The Austrian-born architect said, "It is in the great tradition of the guillotine." Its tilting, slablike sections invert traditional setbacks, overlapping and sliding over each other so that they appear to be at risk of slipping off the building like an avalanche. Abraham grew up in the Tyrolean Alps, and his familiarity with the region's jagged cliff sides and massively fortified stone farmhouses is evident here.

The tilted façade exaggerates the convergence lines of perspective, making the distances seem much greater so that the building looks like a skyscraper in miniature. Its slippery setbacks add just the touch of vertigo needed for a tall building. The proportions of the 25-foot base compared to the height also make the building appear much taller than it is.

Anthropomorphic metaphors are nearly impossible to escape in describing the zinc-and-glass surfaced building's physiognomy. Seen from the street, especially in profile, the façade resembles a primitive mask with deep punctured slots like an early Picasso sculpture or an ancient Greek helmet. The architect himself uses body-related terms to describe the parti: the heavy glass façade is the mask, the structure and interior space are the core, and the sculptural zigzagging concrete fire stairs to the rear are the vertebrae. The different anatomical pieces are also meant to represent qualities of architecture: the vertebrae are lift or ascension, the core is support, and the mask is suspension.

The forum was built as a high-visibility showpiece for Austrian culture, but Abraham rejects any cozy associations with Viennese finger cookies or similar ornate symbols. His building is a deliberate atavism to early forms of modernism, the industrial design of the Secessionist Movement, whose starkly angular geometries were so much a matrix of twentieth-century architecture.

Abraham emphasizes construction above all, and the strongly expressed structure clearly shows the influence of the building's structural engineers, Ove Arup & Partners. The glass curtain is used for its weight and thickness rather than its transparency, but the structural cross-beams are clearly visible through the glass. They seem to press outward against the buildings to either side. Zinc sections bump out from the glass surface like deeply incised stone carvings. Despite the building's impenetrable front, one of its projections looks from the side very much like a magnified chunk of an International Style glass curtain wall stuck onto the sloping plane of the façade. The tension between the two equates steel-and-glass construction with more primitive stone building.

Blocky stone sections correspond to three different uses: the rectangle of the director's office juts out at the eighth floor; the middle section houses a small, wood-paneled performance space for film and music; and the top is an extraordinary four-level apartment for the director and his family. Public exhibition galleries occupy a below-grade space, the street level, and a mezzanine. The floor space of the entire building is an exiguous 33,000 square feet.

Inside the grim visage of this tower beats the icy heart of a Norn maiden. Materials of glass, steel, and brushed aluminum give the lobby an almost clinical feel. The exhibit spaces are narrow, crammed around the giant stainless steel drum of the elevator core. But at the same time everything seems to float weightlessly. Gorgeous bluestone paving runs throughout the lobby and up the stairs, hovering over a stainless steel gutter on one side and empty space on the other.

As if to compensate for the ponderous construction and defensive aspect of the exterior, the interior is as free-flowing and airy as its narrow space allows. A rear skylight throws light over the lobby. The mezzanine goes one step beyond the floating planes of Mies's Barcelona Pavilion to merely suggest spatial divisions with waist-high planes of glass secured below the stone flooring, creating almost the Platonic idea of a wall. There are some lovely illusionistic details: the turned ends of the tubular metal handrails stop just short of touching the walls, as if defying gravity.

By building something brutish and challenging, rather than attractive and easy, Abraham has thrown a gauntlet to future New York architects to go beyond conventional design.

[1] The interior of the Austrian Cultural Forum is a severe exercise in minimalism, with a "barely there" floating staircase.

Westin New York at Times Square

270 WEST 43RD STREET » ARQUITECTONICA, 2002

DESIGNED BY the Miami-based firm Arquitectonica, the colorful, bifurcated 45-story, 532-foot-tall Westin Hotel looks like nothing else on the Manhattan skyline and was treated like a rank upstart by New York critics. The *New York Times* called it an "outsider," but celebrated it as a breath of Latin modernism. The *New Yorker* observed scathingly, "The glass must be the ugliest curtain in New York."

But Laurinda Spear, half of the Arquitectonica team along with her husband Bernardo Fort-Brescia, says the critics got it all wrong. "The Westin had nothing to do with Miami, nothing to do with 'Latin,' and everything to do with that particular site," she insists. "My mentor, Robert A. M. Stern, was with us at every stage of the development."

The Westin stands out because it dares to use color—lots of it—in the city that cultivated the monochrome green-glass International Style curtain wall. Colors, especially the sky-blue and copper tones chosen by the architects, seemed to some too upsetting against the general pigeon-gray background. The color scheme works best under atmospheric conditions rarely seen in New York—blue skies and flawless sunsets that occur all the time . . . in Miami.

The western façade is silvery-blue decorated with vertical stripes of bright blue, purple, and lavender that the architects refer to as "brushstrokes," while the slightly shorter tower to the east is covered in coppery glass with horizontal bands of blue and brown. An illuminated glass arc streaks between the two sections and lights up like a searchlight at a Hollywood premiere at night. Rather than applying electronics to the surface like most other architects of Times Square buildings, Arquitectonica chose to incorporate the sign within the structure itself.

An unusually shaped, 17-story "bustle" clad in colored steel panels brings the 863-room hotel down to street level on the Eighth Avenue front. The bustle looks like a child's cartoon

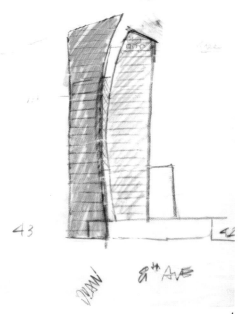

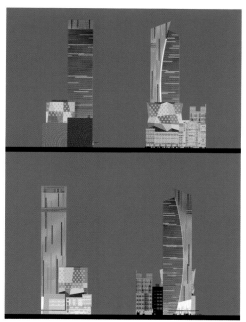

1

2

3

[1] The original parti of the Westin suggests earth and sky split by a comet's trail. [2] The elevations of the building are as variegated as its surroundings. [3] Details of the lobby, including wood paneling and strip lighting in the ceiling, reflect details of the exterior.

drawing of a building in its outline, palette, and fenestration. The top and sides are saw-toothed as if they had been cut with pinking shears, and the structure is kinked at the waistline, so that the windows pitch upward and downward. Like 42nd Street itself, the hotel is meant to disorient you a little. The peas-and-carrots pattern of jagged geometric swatches is punctuated by an odd detail—casement windows that look like ordinary sash windows. Guests inside peer out, as amazed as the pedestrians are to see them.

The building's base is a test of one's tolerance for overload. It is simply impossible to keep the whole picture in view; it is like trying to size up the great distance between a golf ball and the hole—you would need eyes placed like a goat's. All manner of ungodly junk is affixed to the most dominant corner at 42nd and Eighth: a giant lava lamp with moving globules, three-story letters "NY" in sequins that shimmer in the breeze, restaurant signs, an electronic zipper, and billboards for the latest Hollywood block-busters playing at the E-Walk multiplex are all incorporated into the base. For tourists arriving by bus at the Port Authority terminal cater-corner across the street, this permanent Mardi Gras float is their first image of the big city.

The high rise's most pleasing aspect is its parti—the way the squat, bulky base plays off against the sweeping arc of the tower. It is rare to see so much sky around a Manhattan tower, and the Westin uses the open space to maximum advantage. The effect is a kind of tarted-up post-modern relative to her more prim and proper Park Avenue sister, Lever House.

The architects pull a turnabout inside, with a sober glass-walled International Style lobby and atrium, as if to show they can play at

2

that game, too. Here, the striped motif is carried out monochromatically in strips of shiny black and white marble set in gray granite. There are many elegant details throughout—the principal motif is picked up in the pastel colors of the elevator banks, recessed copper-colored ceiling lights, and in the rugs and an etched glass screen designed by Spear.

The sense of luxury requisite for a $300 million hotel is conveyed through its materials. Burnished, geometrically angled wooden paneling behind the reception area echoes the serrated edges of the bustle in warm, rich tones. The quiet little Bar 10 is paneled in extraordinary, creamy teakwood stone from Pakistan, and the floors are zebrawood.

Still, the atrium is not quite grand or spacious enough. There is a lot of wasted space. The zigzag mezzanine balcony is little more than an elaborate gangway to the bar, and the big potted plants only serve to highlight the problem, making one think of Frank Lloyd Wright's observation that doctors can bury their mistakes but architects can only plant vines.

[1] The Westin stands out in the Manhattan skyline because of its bold use of color. [2] The elevators carry through the hotel's brightly striped motifs.

Time Warner Building

1 CENTRAL PARK WEST » DAVID CHILDS, 2004

1

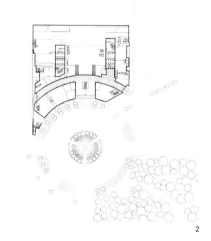

2

DAVID CHILDS may be the most self-effacing star architect at work on the New York skyline. He is nothing if not contextual. His 53-story, 750-foot-tall twin-towered Time Warner Building pays tribute to nearly every element in its environs, providing a transition from the glassy office slabs of midtown to the lower, masonry apartment buildings of the residential Upper West Side.

The parti is itself contextual. The parallelogram-shaped towers reflect the diagonal swath that Broadway cuts across the street grid, while the thick, arced stone base conforms to Columbus Circle. The finials are a tribute to modernist apartments such as the Century that line Central Park West.

Sited between two neighborhoods with distinct functions, the building creates a sympathetic dialog between height and horizontality. Because of the towers' acute and oblique angles, the masses appear to shift depending on from where they are seen. From certain viewpoints, reflexive angles make the towers appear stubby and proportionate to their base, but as perspective shifts, the façade appears to be thin, almost evanescent sheets of glass. This effect is optimized when driving through Columbus Circle. From across the park, the towers appear like slate-colored mirrors reflecting the sky.

Such responsiveness to the site has gone in and out of favor in modernism's checkered history. Columbus Circle itself once provided both extremes—the Coliseum convention center that once stood where the Time Warner is now was a Robert Moses–era monolith that turned a windowless brick wall on the park. Edward Durell Stone's oddly charming Venetian turret, originally the Gallery of Modern Art at 2 Columbus Circle, was once mocked for daring to throw in a curved line, but is now an endangered cause celebre among modernist preservationists.

[1] Cornering the market: the Time Warner Building brings an abundance of shopping to an underutilized corner of the city.

[2] The building's footprint conforms to Columbus Circle.

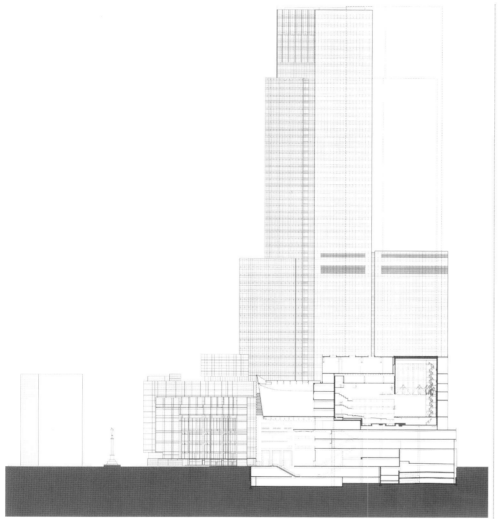

2

Childs wisely celebrates the Central Park site with a supersized show window, which also symbolizes the building's function as a high-end shopping center. This is event architecture—visitors become acutely aware of the volume of the atrium and the vista of the park through the window that fills the entire lobby. The best special effect is found riding the escalator up from the subterranean Whole Foods supermarket, an experience in pure Romantic ascension, rising effortlessly into the sky like a Valkyrie.

Childs's personal touch appears to be a Frank Lloyd Wright–like treatment of floating planes, but with a Darth Vader leadenness. Seen from deep within the building, the massive floor plates hover weightlessly on walls of glass, but at the same time there is something dark and oppressive about them, as if they do not let in enough light. Even the Wrightian built-in planters on the south façade seem to have a wicked edge.

The Time Warner Building is at heart corporate architecture, designed to move goods, and there is something soulless behind its glossy lobby. Though enlivened with reflections from glass and polished surfaces, the space itself is not all that inviting. After taking in the view from an upper balcony, or lounging on one of the Mies Barcelona chairs (a nice touch of luxury), there is little to engage the attention beyond the glittering distractions of the interior shop windows.

[1] The Time Warner Building's stone base contrasts with its ethereal glass towers. [2] The open atrium faces on the statue of Christopher Columbus and leads to shops above and below street level.

Bloomberg Tower

731 LEXINGTON AVENUE » CESAR PELLI, 2004

1

ONE THING Cesar Pelli, who designed the World Financial Center, excels at is delivering a maximum amount of commercial space. The Bloomberg Building and its integrated tower of 105 condominiums is an enormous building—1.25 million square feet (more than 20 percent of one of the original World Trade Center towers, by comparison).

Occupying the entire block bordered by East 58th and East 59th streets and Lexington and Third avenues, the building's bulk is diminished by a clever distribution of volumes. A slender, 55-story tower with an illuminated glass crown that brings it to 849 feet stands with its narrower façade facing Lexington Avenue. An 85-foot-tall base unites the tower with an 8-story podium on Third Avenue, separated by a block-through porte-cochere with a 7-story conical glass-walled atrium that is the showpiece of the composition.

The building is a microcosm of Midtown pushed skyward, seemingly by sheer real-estate pressure. The base is given over to retail; the tower is framed in steel up to the 30th floor to provide office space, largely as the headquarters of multimillionaire Mayor Michael Bloomberg's financial information company; while the 30th

to 54th floors are made of cast-in-place, flat-plate concrete to provide 10-to-12-foot ceiling heights for luxury condominiums.

Pelli, like his fellow corporate architects David Childs and Costas Kondylis, provides a style that by now could be labeled traditional postmodernism. Their buildings are solidly grounded in the modernist tradition, rather than flying in the face of it. They provide eminently practical programs and just enough commentary on the history of modernism to create a critical distance. In the Bloomberg Building, Pelli not only shows he is up to date with the latest curving computer-generated lines of the conical atrium, but also provides the simpler pleasure of reflecting on the nature of steel-and-glass construction. Horizontal window bands of tinted blue glass are separated by narrow white spandrels covering floor plates that resemble plain steel I-beams. In the corners of the setbacks, reflections of the I-beams seem to form steel latticeworks suspended in the sky. The effect expresses the "truth of construction" in the modernist tradition, but adds a postmodern illusion of symbolic reflections rather than actual structure. Retro shallow setbacks add to the tower's sense of height.

Pelli admixes symbols of commercial and residential architecture, befitting the tower's dual nature. Seen one way, the I-beams resemble raw office-tower construction, but from another point of view they are in the tradition of belt courses that marked off floors of apartments in what were once called "French flats," so that the individual tenant could have a sense of townhouse-like ownership. The profile of the tower is clean-lined where the bands of windows meet with simple mullions but at the same time looks rather bumpy compared to its neighbors—from certain angles the I-beams resemble rows of clapboard.

The bar for luxury living in Manhattan keeps getting raised higher, so the Bloomberg condominiums, called One Beacon Court, not

only provide layouts by a world-renowned architect, but interiors by French designer Jacques Grange. The kitchens feature Brazilian granite floors and restaurant-style refrigerators, while the baths have marble counters and custom maple cabinets. Known for his eclectic mix of classical and modernist elements, Grange finished the interiors in Tuscan pastels to counter the cool glass exterior. The setbacks function as spectacular mullioned extensions of the living rooms, a conflation of bay window and corner office.

The Bloomberg Building has a significant impact on the East Side skyline because of its full-block site and the lower-lying neighboring buildings. Pelli said he was pleased to see that his sky-blue tower was visible from across Central Park, but the architect is contextual in a gentlemanly way: the height of the Third Avenue retail podium acknowledges its neighbor Bloomingdale's, while the nautically trim bands of blue and white are the inverse of the Citicorp Center a few blocks down the avenue and akin to Helmut Jahn's 425 Lexington Avenue. Even the elliptical atrium is related to the granite-columned drum in front of 135 East 57th Street, which frames the tower like a bull's-eye.

[1] The Bloomberg Tower features a seven-story canoidal, or sloping elliptical, atrium.

Freedom Tower

CHURCH TO WEST STREETS AND LIBERTY TO VESEY STREETS »

DAVID CHILDS, DANIEL LIBESKIND, 2008

THE FREEDOM TOWER, the centerpiece of the World Trade Center restoration, has gone through many permutations but as of this writing still remains a shimmering mirage on the drawing board. This much is definite: the spire of the tower will reach the symbolic height of 1,776 feet, representing the country's date of independence, and the building itself will be 70 stories tall. The top three stories will contain an observation deck and restaurants. The tower's asymmetrical spire recalls the torch of the Statue of Liberty, and its open-work steel construction works on several levels as a representation of strength, a contextual reference to the suspension cables of the Brooklyn Bridge, and a ghostly evocation of the original towers. Libeskind says his concept of the open fretwork of the tower "includes the world of the sky above. It becomes this very open, ethereal building that lets light right through it."

David Childs's 52-story, 750-foot-tall 7 World Trade Center was the first to be under construction after the attack. Its 10-level base, which houses a Con Ed substation, was conceived of as a stainless steel block from which a 45-foot-high lobby is carved. The developer Larry A. Silverstein put a premium on safety, so the glass façade is made from shatterproof glass similar to automobile windshields, and the core is cast-in-place concrete instead of the former towers' steel and drywall core, which melted from the heat of the explosion after the terrorist attack.

The master plan for the site has a convoluted history. The original developer's proposal was rejected as uninspired. Then an open competition was held between master architects. United Architects' plan showed a group of torqued towers leaning into each other as if they were giving a group hug. "The structural concept for the towers has been developed with the intention of establishing a new tower typology," the group declared. Norman Foster weighed in

with paired 1,764-foot towers that touched at different points, looking either as if they were kissing, like the well-known Brancusi sculpture, or knock-kneed. A consortium of Richard Meier, Peter Eisenman, Charles Gwathmey, and Steven Holl designed two provocative, interlocking towers set at right angles like multiplied stacks of the letter H, with airy "skyway" concourses at different levels.

Libeskind's more conventional design with its historical connotations won the day. In commemorating tragedy, there is a pull towards tradition and the past, to create a sense of continuity. This is one reason why Maya Lin's minimalist design for the Vietnam Memorial was so controversial, and veterans demanded a representational monument of human figures to stand beside it.

Further internecine wrangling followed. Silverstein, who owns the lease to the site, wanted to bring his own architect, David Childs, aboard to design the Freedom Tower. It was agreed that Libeskind would remain the master planner and his general guidelines and placement of the tower would be followed, but specifics for the central symbolic skyscraper would be left to Childs. They were a Mutt and Jeff pairing from the beginning—Libeskind is five feet three inches, mercurial, European, dressed all in black, while Childs is tall, tweedy, and stolidly American.

Many features of the 16-acre site have been determined: Fulton and Greenwich streets will be reconnected to run through what was an unused, windblown superblock. "The superblock was a bad moment in the 1960s," Childs says. "Being able to connect neighborhoods is very different from Yamasaki's program. There will be views, corridors, access to buildings." Libeskind agrees that "there will be the connectivity of life on the site to all the spaces in between. The spaces will have a human scale that offers intimacy and also grandeur."

The commemorative site will include an

exposed section of the slurry wall that formed the foundation of the original towers and the "Wedge of Light," a space between the buildings that marks the position of the sun during the time the towers were hit and collapsed. The footprints of the buildings will feature pedestrian ramps leading 30 feet below ground level to pools of water as part of a memorial called *Reflecting Absence* by Michael Arad and the landscape architect Peter Walker. Frank Gehry has been awarded the contract for a new center to make the complex even more of an architectural destination.

The jewel in the crown will be Santiago Calatrava's World Trade Center Path Station that alights like a dove of peace at the base of the center. The columnless, underground space will be larger than the great room of Grand Central Terminal. Its glass-and-steel ribbed retractable canopy will play off the Freedom Tower's skeletal steeple.

The task of designing at Ground Zero is more than replacing the old towers, according to Libeskind. "I see it as a new neighborhood that is being created," he says. "Nobody really needs skyscrapers, but there is something visceral and spiritual to put yourself at risk from the cosmos. That part of New York is not whimsical, and it is something deeply rooted in why people come to New York."

1

[1] The open fretwork spire of the Freedom Tower will in part be an homage to the cables of the Brooklyn Bridge.

Adler, Jerry. *High Rise: How 1,000 Men and Women Worked Around the Clock for Five Years and Lost $200 Million Building a Skyscraper*. New York: HarperCollins, 1993.

Balfour, Alan. *Rockefeller Center: Architecture as Theater*. New York: McGraw-Hill, 1978.

Bollack, Françoise, and Tom Killian. *Ely Jacques Kahn: New York Architect*. New York: Acanthus Press, 1995.

Cannell, Michael. *I. M. Pei: Mandarin of Modernism*. New York: Carol Southern Books, 1995.

Cohen, Jean-Louis. *Scenes of the World to Come: European Architecture and the American Challenge, 1893–1960*. Paris: Flammarion; and Montréal: Canadian Centre for Architecture, 1995.

Colpitt, Frances. *Minimal Art: The Critical Perspective*. Seattle: The University of Washington Press, 1993.

Diamonstein, Barbaralee. *The Landmarks of New York II*. New York: Harry N. Abrams, 1993.

Dolkart, Andrew S., and New York City Landmarks Preservation Commission. *Guide to New York City Landmarks*. New York: John Wiley & Sons, 1998.

Dudley, George A. *A Workshop for Peace: Designing the United Nations Headquarters*. Cambridge, Mass.: MIT Press, 1994.

Fahr-Becker, Gavriel. *Wiener Werkstäte: 1903–1932*. Cologne: Taschen, 1995.

Federal Writers' Project of the Works Progress Administration in New York City. *The WPA Guide to New York City: The Federal Writers' Project Guide to 1930s New York*. Reprint, New York: New Press, 1995.

Ferriss, Hugh. *The Metropolis of Tomorrow*. Reprint, New York: Princeton Architectural Press, 1986.

Fried, Michael. *Art and Objecthood*. Chicago: The University of Chicago Press, 1998.

Goldberger, Paul. *The Skyscraper*. New York: Alfred A. Knopf, 1981.

Goldman, Jonathan. *The Empire State Building Book*. New York: St. Martin's Press, 1980.

Hall, Peter, ed. *Tibor Kalman: Perverse Optimimst*. New York: Princeton Architectural Press, 1998.

Hitchcock, Henry-Russell, and Philip Johnson. *The International Style*. New York: W. W. Norton, 1996.

Huxtable, Ada Louise. *The Tall Building Artistically Reconsidered: The Search for a Skyscraper Style*. Berkeley: University of California Press, 1992.

James, Warren A., ed. *Kohn Pedersen Fox: Architecture and Urbanism 1986–1992*. New York: Rizzoli, 1993.

Koolhaas, Rem. *Delirious New York: A Retroactive Manifesto for Manhattan*. New York: Monacelli Press, 1994.

Koolhaas, Rem, and Bruce Mau. *S,M,L,XL*. New York: Monacelli Press, 1995.

Kreimeier, Klaus. *The Ufa Story: A History of Germany's Greatest Film Company, 1918–1945*. New York: Hill and Wang, 1996.

Krinsky, Carol Herselle. *Gordon Bunshaft of Skidmore, Owings & Merrill*. Cambridge, Mass.: MIT Press, 1988.

Landau, Sarah Bradford, and Carl W. Condit. *Rise of the New York Skyscraper: 1865–1913*. New Haven, Conn.: Yale University Press, 1996.

Le Corbusier. *Towards a New Architecture*. Reprint, Mineola, N.Y.: Dover Publications, 1986.

Lewis, Hilary, and John O'Connor. *Philip Johnson: The Architect in His Own Words*. New York: Rizzoli, 1994.

Long, Rose-Carol Washton, ed. *German Expressionism: Documents from the End of the Wilhelmine Empire to the Rise of National Socialism*. Berkeley: University of California Press, 1993.

Morrone, Francis. *The Architectural Guidebook to New York City*. Salt Lake City, Utah: Gibbs Smith Publisher, 1994.

Nash, Eric. *New York's 50 Best Secret Architectural Treasures*. New York: City & Company, 1996.

Nash, Eric. *New York's 50 Best Skyscrapers*. New York: City & Company, 1997.

Newhouse, Victoria. *Wallace K. Harrison, Architect*. New York: Rizzoli, 1989.

O'Brian, John, ed. *Clement Greenberg: The Collected Essays and Criticism, Vol. 4, Modernism with a Vengeance, 1957–1969*. Chicago: University of Chicago Press, 1993.

Pelli, Cesar. *Cesar Pelli: Buildings and Projects, 1965–1990*. New York: Rizzoli, 1990.

Reynolds, Donald Martin. *The Architecture of New York City: Histories and Views of Important Structures, Sites, and Symbols*. New York: John Wiley & Sons, 1994.

Robins, Anthony. *The World Trade Center*. Englewood, Fla.: Pineapple Press; and Fort Lauderdale, Fla.: Omnigraphics, 1987.

Ruttenbaum, Steven. *Mansions in the Clouds: The Skyscraper Palazzi of Emery Roth*. New York: Balsam Press, 1986.

Sabbagh, Karl. *Skyscraper: The Making of a Building*. Reprint, New York: Viking, 1990.

Schleier, Merrill. *The Skyscraper in American Art: 1890–1931*. New York: Da Capo Press, 1990.

Stern, Robert A. M., Gregory Gilmartin, and John Montague Massengale. *New York 1900: Metropolitan Architecture and Urbanism, 1890–1915*. New York: Rizzoli, 1983.

Stern, Robert A. M., Gergory Gilmartin, and Thomas Mellins. *New York 1930: Architecture and Urbanism Between the Two World Wars*. New York: Rizzoli, 1987.

Stern, Robert A. M., Thomas Mellins, and David Fishman. *New York 1960: Architecture and Urbanism Between the Second World War and the Bicentennial*. New York: Monacelli Press, 1995.

Sussman, Elisabeth. *City of Ambition: Artists & New York, 1900–1960*. New York: Whitney Museum of American Art; and Paris: Flammarion, 1996.

Tauranac, John. *The Empire State Building: The Making of a Landmark*. New York: St. Martin's Press, 1996.

Thomsen, Christian W. *Visionary Architecture from Babylon to Virtual Reality*. John William Gabriel, trans. Munich and New York: Prestel-Verlag, 1994.

Thorndike, Joseph J., Jr., ed. *Three Centuries of Notable American Architects*. New York: American Heritage, 1981.

Tunick, Susan. *Terra-Cotta Skyline*. New York: Princeton Architectural Press, 1997.

van Leeuwen, Thomas A. P. *The Skyward Trend of Thought*. Cambridge, Mass.: MIT Press, 1988.

Willensky, Elliot, and Norval White. *AIA Guide to New York City*. San Diego: Harcourt Brace Jovanovich, 1988.

Willis, Carol. *Form Follows Finance: Skyscrapers and Skylines in New York and Chicago*. New York: Princeton Architectural Press, 1995.

Willis, Carol, ed. *Building the Empire State*. New York: W. W. Norton, 1998.

Zaknic, Ivan. *The Final Testament of Père Corbu: A Translation and Interpretation of* Mise au Point. New Haven, Conn.: Yale University Press, 1997.

ACANTHUS LEAF: a conventionalized leafy design characteristic of the Corinthian order

ADDORSED: a symmetrical motif in which the figures are set back-to-back

AFFRONTED: a symmetrical motif in which the figures are face-to-face

ARCADE: a line of arches and supporting columns

ARCHITECTURE PARLANT: a style of architecture that expresses its purpose with overt symbolism

ART DECO: a design style popularized at the 1925 Exposition Internationale des Arts Décoratifs et Industriels Modernes in Paris and characterized by streamlined, two-dimensional figures and a machine aesthetic

ART MODERNE: a Depression-era style that emphasized simple streamlines

ASHLAR: smooth, square stones laid in straight courses; random ashlar has a more haphazard pattern

ASTYLAR: columnless

ATTIC: the decorative crown of a building

AXONOMETRIC: a three-sided representation of a solid object

BALUSTRADE: a railing supported by small posts

BARREL VAULT: a tunnel-like vault in the form of a half cylinder

BAS-RELIEF: sculpture that projects only slightly from the surface

BAUHAUS: a German design school, 1919–1932, that emphasized structuralism and the use of industrial materials

BAY: a grouping of windows

BEAUX-ARTS: a classically inspired style taught by the École Nationale Supérieure des Beaux-Arts in Paris in the nineteenth century, characterized by symmetry, balance, and clarity of function

BELTCOURSE: a projecting horizontal course of masonry

BLIND: having no opening

BRACKET: an architectural support projecting from a wall; see corbel

BRICOLAGE: a postmodern technique of assembling disparate elements into a pattern that forms a new meaning

BRISE-SOLEIL: an awning-like device used by Le Corbusier

BUTTRESS: an exterior masonry mass that helps support the lateral thrust of the walls

CAMPANILE: a bell tower, especially a free-standing one

CANTILEVERED: a projecting structure supported at only one end

CARTOUCHE: a decorative oval seal

CARYATID: a supporting column in the form of a female figure

CHAMFERED: beveled, usually cut on a 45-degree angle

CHEVRON: a V-shaped motif

CLASSICAL: referring to the styles of ancient Greece and Rome

CLASSICAL REVIVAL: styles influenced by Greek and Roman design

COFFERED: a ceiling decorated with sunken panels

COLONETTE: a thin column

COLONNADE: a line of columns

COPING: the top layer of a wall

CORE: the central service functions of a building, including elevators, electricity, and plumbing

CORINTHIAN: the most elaborate of the three orders of Greek architecture, characterized by columns with ornate capitals decorated with acanthus leaves

CORNICE: a horizontal molding that projects from the top of a wall or building

COSMATESQUE: polychromatic marble mosaic work from the Romanesque period

CRENELLATION: a notch, as in a battlement

CUPOLA: a small dome

CURTAIN WALL: a non-load-bearing wall that clads the structure

DADO: a decorative lower part of a wall

DECONSTRUCTIONISM: a postmodern style that contradicts structuralism

DENTILED: decorated with a series of small rectangular blocks that project like teeth

DIAPERING: a flat, gridded pattern

DORIC: the oldest Greek order, characterized by heavy columns with simple capitals

DORMER: a vertical window in a sloping roof

DRUM: a circular wall that supports a dome

ECHINATED: decorated with an egg and dart molding

ECLECTIC: a nineteenth- and early-twentieth-century style that freely sampled from historic periods

EGG-AND-DART MOLDING: a stylized, classical banded ornament said to represent egg yolks and birds' talons

ELL: an addition at a right angle to the main part of a building

ENGAGED COLUMN: a column that is not entirely free-standing

ENTASIS: use of a slight curve to counteract the illusion of sagging in vertical elements

ESQUISSE: a sketch, especially of a building's parti

FAÇADE: the main exterior of a building

FAÏENCE: glazed tile

FEDERAL STYLE: an American style from 1780–1820, typified by low, pitched roofs; large glass areas; and simplified Georgian symmetry

FENESTRATION: the arrangement and treatment of windows

FLUTED: having long, rounded grooves

FLYING BUTTRESS: an open-arched buttress typical of Gothic architecture

FRETWORK: decorative carving typical of classical design

FUNCTIONALISM: an often-misinterpreted design philosophy in which the form of an object is subjugated to its use

GARGOYLE: a grotesque projecting ornament in Gothic design

GARLAND: a wreath or leaf decoration

GEORGIAN STYLE: an English style (1714–76) with an emphasis on symmetry and enriched classical detailing

GERMAN EXPRESSIONISM: an early-twentieth-century style characterized by bizarre, disorienting angles and lighting, influenced by German silent cinema

GIRDER: a large, usually horizontal beam

GLOIRE: a sunburst pattern characteristic of rococo design

GOTHIC: a medieval style of elaborately detailed, perpendicular architecture

GREEK REVIVAL: a simplified classical revival style (1750–1860) influenced by the purity of Greek classical architecture

GRIFFIN: an ornamental figure of a half-lion, half-eagle

GUASTAVINO TILE: a sturdy, lightweight clay tile developed by the architect Rafael Guastavino

HEADER: the narrow end of a brick

HISTORICIST: use of a style when it is no longer current

HORTUS: a room in a traditional Roman household

HVAC: acronym for heating, ventilation, and air-conditioning system

I BEAM: a steel beam that looks like the letter I in cross section

INFILL: a building on a midblock site rather than free-standing

INTERNATIONAL STYLE: a mid-twentieth-century style that emphasized structure, volume, and mass over symbolic ornament

INTRADOS: the inner curve of an arch

IONIC: a Greek order distinguished by slender columns topped by capitals with volutes

LIGHT COURT: a shallow, window-lined courtyard built to let light into interior spaces

LOGGIA: an arcaded gallery

LOMBARD REVIVAL: a style influenced by northern Italian Romanesque architecture

MANSARD: a roof with two slopes

MASK: a representation of a face on a building

MASTABA: an Egyptian structure with a flat roof and sloping sides

MINIMALISM: an aesthetic that reduces architecture to its most essential forms and materials

MODERN CLASSICISM: a term used in the 1920s for what is now called Art Deco

MODERNISM: a twentieth-century style that moved away from historicism and symbolic representation toward a purer use of volume, form, and mass

MOLDING: projecting or sunken ornamental contours

MULLIONS: slender vertical divisions between window panes

NEO-BAROQUE: an early-twentieth-century revival style mainly used in theaters

NEO-RENAISSANCE: a Renaissance revival style

OBELISK: a four-sided pillar that tapers to a pyramid

OCULUS: a round window or opening at the top of a dome; pl. oculi

ORIEL: a bay window corbeled out from a wall

OX-EYE: a round aperture

PALAZZO: a Renaissance Italian mansion

PARAPET: part of a wall that projects above the roof

PARTI: a building's overall design or concept

PARTY WALL: a wall that adjoins a separate structure

PEDIMENT: the decorative triangular gable above a façade.
broken pediment: a pediment in which the cornice is split in the center

PERISTYLE: a row of columns inside the courtyard of a Roman household

PICTURESQUE: a nineteenth-century style that emphasizes color and composition

PIER: a long vertical element in a façade

PILASTER: a stylized flat column

PILOTI: a stilt-like column

PINNACLE: a small turret, common in Gothic architecture

PLATFORM: the base of a building

PLINTH: the base of a column

PLINTH BLOCK: a flat, plain element at the base of a column

POLYCHROME: using many colors

POSTMODERN: a style that rejects the structuralism and unity of modernism in favor of a readoption of historicism and discontinuous symbolic expression

PUTTI: cherubs

QUOIN: a large, square stone that marks a building corner

RENAISSANCE: European architecture between 1400 and 1600 that emphasizes humanist scale, symmetry, and use of classical orders

RETARDATAIRE: a French term meaning "backdated" or using an outmoded style

REVEAL: the visible thickness of a wall between its surface and a door or window

REVIVAL: a style that draws inspiration from an earlier historical style

ROCK-FACED: the unworked, natural surface of stone

ROCOCO: ornately wrought

ROMANESQUE: a style influenced by European architecture of the eleventh and twelfth centuries, emphasizing round arches and thick masonry

ROSETTE: a conventionalized floral motif

ROUNDEL: a circular decorative motif

ROUND-HEADED: ending in a semicircle

RUE CORRIDOR: the traditional cornice lines and façades of a street

RUSTICATION: stone cut in large blocks with an unfinished surface and deeply recessed joints

SCROLL: an S-shaped ornament

SEGMENTAL: an arc that is less than a semicircle

SEJANT: in heraldry, a sitting animal

SETBACK: a building profile in which the upper stories are smaller than the base

SOFFIT: the horizontal underside of an eaves or cornice

SPANDREL: the wall space between the top of a window and the sill of the window above it

STADTKRÖNE: German, literally "crown of the city," derived from the Gothic cathedral as the symbol of a city

STATANT: in heraldry, a beast standing on all its feet

STEEL CAGE OR STEEL SKELETON FRAME: a construction method pioneered in Chicago in the late 1800s, in which an internally connected steel frame supports the weight of a building, rather than exterior walls; it is the basic design of most modern office buildings

STRINGCOURSE: a decorative horizontal course in a wall

STRUCTURALISM: an aesthetic in which a building expresses how it is constructed

STYLOBATE: a base for a row of columns

SURBASE: the border at the top of a baseboard

TERRA COTTA: a decorative, lightweight building material made of heated clay

TRABEATED: built with posts and beams rather than arches

TRAVERTINE: a warmly colored, porous marble

TURRET: a small tower

VOLUTE: a spiral scroll used in column capitals

VOUSSOIR: a wedge-shaped stone in an arch

WIENER WERKSTÄTTE: a Viennese art movement (1903–32) that emphasized abstract geometric designs in the fine and applied arts

WING: an extension to the main part of a building

ZIGGURAT: a stepped-back pyramid

ZONING CODE OF 1916: a municipal code that required the upper stories of building to step back from the street front according to a formula, in order to allow greater penetration of air and sunlight; the code was catalytic in changing skyscraper design

ZONING CODE OF 1961: a change in the code that led to the formulation of towers in a plaza, in which builders received height tradeoffs for providing public amenities such as parks and subway improvements

PHOTOGRAPHS

Images are identified by page number. When more
than one image appears on a page, the corre-
sponding image number is given in parentheses.

All full-size photographs at the beginning of each
essay except for that on page 190 are copyright
© Norman McGrath, all rights reserved.
Additional photographs by Norman McGrath:
ii, viii, xii–xiii, xiv, 9, 11 (1), 15, 21 (1), 25 (3), 27
(1), 29, 33 (1), 65 (3), 69 (2), 71, 76 (4), 79 (3),
83 (2), 87 (1, 2), 94 (1), 99 (1), 101, 105, 113 (1),
134, 135 (2), 139 (1), 141, 143 (2, 3), 155 (3), 159 (3),
163, 164, 169 (1), 171, 173 (2), 174, 175, 179, 186,
189, 199

Archive Photos/PNI: 100

Arquitectonica: 181 (1, 2)

Arquitectonica, photo by John Gosling RTKL: 182

Arquitectonica, photo by Norman McGrath: 183

Arquitectonica, photo by Nacasa & Partners: 181 (3)

Sylvie Ball: 3 (1), 5 (1), 8, 64

Chase Manhattan Bank: 113 (2, 3, 4)

Collection of Fisk University, Nashville, Tennessee:
31 (2)

Christian de Portzamparc: 169 (2)

Condé Nast Publications, photo by Roger Dong,
2000: 172 (1)

Four Seasons Hotel: 167 (1, 2, 3)

Fox & Fowle Architects: 173 (3)

General Motors Corp.: 123 (1, 2)

Gwathmey Siegel & Associates: 157 (1, 2)

IBM Archives: 145 (1, 2)

Philip Johnson/Alan Ritchie Architects: 147 (1, 2), 151

Kohn Pedersen Fox Associates: 161 (2)

Kohn Pedersen Fox Associates, photo by Michael
Moran: 161 (1)

Library of Congress Prints & Photographs Division:
7, 17 (1), 18 (3), 69 (1), 85 (2)

Library of Congress Prints & Photographs Division,
Architectural Drawings Collection: 17 (2)

Library of Congress Prints & Photographs Division,
Detroit Publishing Company Photograph
Collection: 19, 21 (2)

Library of Congress Prints & Photographs Division,
George Grantham Bain Collection: 13 (1)

Library of Congress Prints & Photographs Division,
Gottscho-Schleisner Collection Magazine
Photograph Collection: 65 (2, 4), 109 (1, 2)

Library of Congress Prints & Photographs Division,
Motion Pictures Posters Collection: 76 (1)

Library of Congress Prints & Photographs Division,
New York World-Telegram and the Sun
Newspaper Photograph Collection: 75, 76 (3)

The McGraw-Hill Companies: 81 (1, 2, 3, 4), 127

MetLife: 13 (2)

Murphy/Jahn: 153 (1, 2, 3)

Collection of the Museum of the City of New York: 1,
3 (2), 11 (2, 3), 13 (3), 23, 25 (1, 2), 27 (2), 33 (2), 35
(1, 2), 37, 39 (1, 2), 43 (1), 47 (1, 2, 3), 49 (1, 2), 51,
53 (1), 57 (2), 59 (3), 61 (2), 63, 73 (2, 3), 79 (1, 2),
85 (1, 3), 89, 97 (1, 2), 99 (2), 103 (2, 3), 106

Eric P. Nash: 5 (2), 59 (1)

New York City Landmarks Preservation Commission:
55 (1, 2), 61 (1), 83 (1)

Collection of the New-York Historical Society: 31 (1,
3), 41, 43 (2, 3), 45, 53 (2), 57 (1), 59 (2), 67, 73 (1),
76 (2), 77 (5, 6), 91, 115 (1, 2)

Pei Cobb Freed & Partners: 119 (1, 2)

John Portman & Associates: 149 (3)

John Portman & Associates, photo by Bo Parker:
149 (1, 2)

Rockefeller Center Archive Center: 93 (1),
94 (2, 3), 95 (4, 5, 6)

Der Scutt Architect: 125 (1, 2, 3), 143 (1)

Skidmore, Owings & Merrill: 103 (1), 111 (2, 3), 121 (2),
131 (1, 2), 155 (1, 2), 159 (1, 2), 185 (1, 2), 187,
190, 191

Alan Schindler: 177

Skyviews: 128

SONY Music: 117 (2)

Ezra Stoller © Esto: 107, 111 (1), 121 (1), 135 (3), 137 (1, 2)

Venator Group: 18 (1, 2)

John Wiley & Sons: 139 (2)

World Financial Properties: 165 (2, 3, 4, 5)

Photo by Richard Wurts, from Stanley Appelbaum,
The New York World's Fair 1939/1940 (Mineola,
NY: Dover, 1977): 129 (2)

Minoru Yamasaki Associates: 133, 135 (3)